RECIPE HALL OF FAME

Guilty
PLEASURES

Fantasy Chocolate Cheesecake, page 71

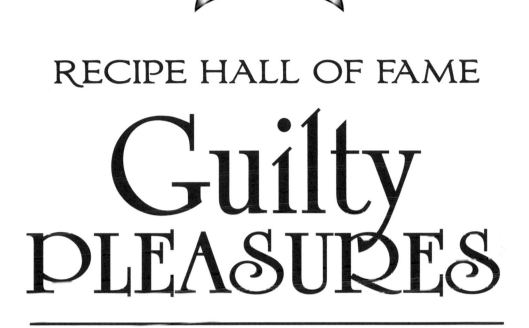

BEST OF THE BEST

RECIPE HALL OF FAME

Guilty PLEASURES

Indulgences to Die For!

Gwen McKee and Barbara Moseley

QUAIL RIDGE PRESS

Preserving America's Food Heritage

To my wonderful little mother, Esther Grace McLin,
whose desserts were legendary . . . and as sweet as she was.

—Gwen McKee

To Mama Jean, who has influenced my life in so many ways,
including what we laughingly refer to as making a mess in the kitchen.
She enjoys a little bite of something sweet after a delicious meal and
after her "nap," but maintains her "girlish" figure at age 96.

—Barbara Moseley

ISBN–13: 978–1-934193-86-0
ISBN–10: 1-934193-86-0

On the front cover: Warm Chocolate Brownie Cups, page 173

On the back cover, clockwise: Cappuccino Flats (page 93), Bourbon Pecan Butterscotch Pie (page 134), The Best Carrot Cake Ever (page 27), and Lime Pecan Bars (page 120)

Front cover photo by Emily Mills Burkett

Photos by Greg Campbell Photography
    Fantasy Chocolate Cheesecake (pages 2 and 71),
    and Chocolate-Covered Cherry Cookies (page 81)

Printed in the United States of America

First edition, November 2012

About the Photography: The food photographs in this book were taken by Gwen McKee
and Quail Ridge Press staff member Emily Mills Burkett (except those mentioned above
by Greg Campbell Photography). All food in the photographs was purchased at ordinary grocery stores and prepared exactly to recipe directions. No artificial food-styling
techniques were used to enhance the food's appearance. Only water was sometimes
spritzed on the food to keep it looking fresh during the photo shoot.

QUAIL RIDGE PRESS
P. O. Box 123 • Brandon, MS 39043
info@quailridge.com • www.quailridge.com
www.facebook.com/cookbookladies

Contents

My Chocolate Cake, page 31

Preface

"Life is just a bowl of cherries."
"If I knew you were coming, I'd a baked a cake."
"Eat pie first . . . life is uncertain."

How many times have you refused a tempting dessert offered to you, only to finally give in and ask for "just a small piece, please"? Or perhaps you have agreed to share a favorite dessert at a restaurant? (Of course, that may be as much about the cost as the calories.) But I look at it this way: If you're going to indulge, you want to be sure it is worth it! Know that what you are preparing for your guests is going to be a surefire winner that all of them will declare most scrumptious, and go home raving about whatever you served.

I have to believe that these sorts of guilty pleasures ought to be around for the times when we absolutely need them. Okay, want. But regardless, Barbara Moseley and I are making no bones about being proud to bring you a "scrumpdillyumptious" collection of downright delicious indulgences in this cookbook. Having been around thousands of cookbooks for more than thirty years, believe me, these fabulous recipes are all *Recipe Hall of Famers*, for sure.

Guilty Pleasures was begun as a baking book, geared around entertaining and the holidays, but we soon realized that baking, to us, said . . .

"Bake a cake."

"Bake cookies."

"Bake a pie."

"Bake something sweet."

. . . more so than it said, "Bake a casserole." And so we left those out.

I have always finished a meal with a dessert. It never is very much, but it is the "icing on the cake," so to speak, and I was raised to expect it.

My sweet little mother, who incidentally lived to be 95, planned her dessert first, then the rest of her meal to go around it. Born and raised in New Orleans, and on its delicious cuisine, her sweet treats were legendary, and were awaited with great anticipation. The care and attention she gave to the baking process, and the magnificent dishes she achieved, instilled in me a standard of excellence that we have endeavored to convey in this cookbook.

Indeed, Mother's scratch cakes were the first to be sold at the school fairs, and she was asked so often to make a cake for assorted special occasions, that when we came home to that delicious aroma in her kitchen, we feared it was not for us—and it often wasn't. But suffice it to say, Mother didn't let us go without dessert of some kind. Nevah!

This cookbook is not meant to tempt you to eat something you think you shouldn't. And for that reason, we have titled it so that you will KNOW there are *Guilty Pleasures* inside. Perhaps you should treat yourself and others only when the occasion calls for it. After all, we don't toast champagne all the time, but I do like to keep a bottle chilled lest an occasion suddenly arises. It's fun to pop the cork to immediate jollity of whatever you are celebrating. Likewise, *Guilty Pleasures* is cause for celebration. It should make you sleep better just knowing so many delicious desserts are right here at your fingertips. For sure, my mother would have thought so.

Remember, STRESSED spelled backwards is DESSERTS.

Gwen McKee

Cakes

Peach-Butter Cake

Peach-Butter Cake

¾ cup butter, softened
1½ cups sugar
3 eggs
1 teaspoon vanilla
1 teaspoon lemon extract
¾ cup buttermilk
½ teaspoon baking powder
½ teaspoon baking soda

¼ teaspoon salt
1 teaspoon nutmeg
1 teaspoon cinnamon
2 tablespoons cocoa
1½ cups all-purpose flour
¾ cup chopped pecans, toasted
1 cup (or more) peach preserves

Cream butter and sugar till fluffy. Add unbeaten eggs. Add flavorings to buttermilk, then add baking powder, baking soda, salt, nutmeg, and cinnamon; add cocoa to flour. Add milk mixture alternately with flour mixture to creamed mixture. Stir in pecans, and mix well. Spoon into 2 (9-inch) square pans that have been buttered and floured. Bake at 375° for 25–35 minutes. Cool, then spread peach preserves between layers for filling, and frost top and sides with Sea-Foam Peach Frosting.

SEA-FOAM PEACH FROSTING:
1 egg white
¾ cup packed brown sugar
Dash of salt
3 tablespoons water

¼ cup peach preserves
½ teaspoon vanilla
¼ cup chopped pecans, toasted

Combine egg white, brown sugar, salt, water, and peach preserves in top of double boiler. Beat with hand mixer 1 minute to blend, then place over rapidly boiling water, and beat constantly for 7 minutes, or till frosting stands in peaks. Remove from water, and add vanilla. Beat till thick enough to spread on cake. Sprinkle with pecans. Serves 8.

Editor's Extra: This is a peachy cocoa spice cake, but also delicious unspiced, without the nutmeg and cinnamon.

Come and Dine (Mississippi)

Cranberry Swirl Cake

2 cups all-purpose flour
½ teaspoon salt
1 teaspoon baking powder
1 teaspoon baking soda
½ stick butter or margarine,
    softened
1 cup sugar

2 eggs
1 cup sour cream
1 teaspoon almond or vanilla
    extract
1 (7-ounce) can whole cranberry
    sauce
½ cup chopped nuts

Preheat oven to 350°. Sift together dry ingredients; set aside. In a large bowl, cream butter; gradually add sugar. With mixer at medium speed, add unbeaten eggs, one at a time. Reduce mixer speed, and alternately add dry ingredients and sour cream, ending with dry ingredients. Add flavoring.

Grease an 8-inch tube pan. Put ⅓ of batter in bottom of pan; swirl ⅓ of the whole cranberry sauce into pan. Add another layer of batter and more cranberry sauce. Add remaining batter; swirl the remaining cranberry sauce on top. Sprinkle nuts on top. Bake for 55 minutes.

TOPPING:

¾ cup powdered sugar
1 tablespoon warm water

½ teaspoon almond or vanilla
    extract

While cake bakes, mix together Topping ingredients in small bowl; set aside. Let cake cool in pan for 10 minutes. Remove cake carefully from pan, and drizzle Topping over it. Serves 10.

California Kosher (California)

Glazed Sponge Cake

1 cup butter or margarine,
  softened
1½ cups sugar
4 eggs, beaten
1 teaspoon vanilla, lemon,
  or almond extract

2 cups all-purpose flour,
  unsifted
½ (21-ounce) can pie filling
  (cherry, blueberry, apple, etc.)

Cream butter and sugar till fluffy. Add eggs a little at a time (3 pourings). Add extract. Blend in flour. Spread batter in well-greased 10½x15½x1-inch pan. Score lightly with knife in 24 squares. Drop a teaspoonful of pie filling in center of each square. Bake at 350° for 30 minutes.

Favorite Island Cookery Book II (Hawaii)

German Apple Cake

3 eggs
1 cup cooking oil
2 cups sugar
1 teaspoon vanilla
2 cups all-purpose flour

2 teaspoons cinnamon
½ teaspoon salt
1 teaspoon baking soda
4 cups raw apples, chopped
1 cup nuts

Beat eggs and oil until foamy. Add sugar and vanilla. Sift together flour, cinnamon, salt and baking soda, and add to sugar mixture. Add apples and nuts; mix well. Bake in 9x13x2-inch pan at 350° for 50–60 minutes.

ICING:
6 ounces cream cheese, softened
3 tablespoons melted butter
1 teaspoon vanilla

1½ cups powdered sugar
  (more, if necessary)

Mix all ingredients together, and ice cake while still hot. Serves 9–12.

Favorite Recipes from Associated Women for Harding (Arkansas)

Missouri Upside Down Cake

Arrange your apple slices prettily into the pan and it will seem like it tastes even more delicious . . . if that is possible.

3 tablespoons butter or margarine	⅓ cup sugar
¾ cup brown sugar	2 eggs
2 cooking apples, peeled and sliced	1 teaspoon vanilla
¼ teaspoon cinnamon	1½ cups all-purpose flour
⅓ cup shortening	2 teaspoons baking powder
	½ teaspoon salt
	⅔ cup milk

Melt butter in a 9-inch round pan. Add brown sugar, and stir until melted. Arrange sliced apples on sugar/butter mixture. Sprinkle cinnamon over apples.

Cream shortening and sugar. Blend in eggs and vanilla, beating thoroughly. Add dry ingredients alternately with milk. Pour over apples in pan. Bake at 350° for 40–45 minutes, or until done. Turn out onto serving plate immediately.

Serve with whipped cream or pistachio ice cream. Yields 6–8 servings.

From the Apple Orchard (Missouri)

Cakes are at their prime when freshly baked, but will keep covered for four or five days—if they last that long. Refrigeration dries cakes out. Only cheesecakes or ones that have mousse or whipped cream frosting need refrigeration (or when your butter cream frosting seems to be melting). Cakes need to be covered. Cupcakes are okay in a bakery box for a day, but wrap the box in plastic wrap for longer storage. A cut cake can be kept moist by adding half an apple to the cake container. You can freeze cakes, too, snugly wrapped.

Missouri Upside Down Cake

Blueberry Cake

3 cups all-purpose flour
1½ cups sugar
1 tablespoon baking powder
⅓ teaspoon salt

½ cup shortening
1 cup plus 2 tablespoons milk
2 eggs
1½ cups blueberries

Sift flour, sugar, baking powder, and salt into a bowl, and mix well. Beat shortening in a mixer bowl until creamy. Add flour mixture alternately with milk. Beat 2 minutes, scraping bowl occasionally. Add eggs. Beat 1 minute. Stir in blueberries. Spoon into a greased 5x9-inch loaf pan. Bake at 350° for 50 minutes or until cake tests done. Cool slightly. Slice, and serve with Hard Sauce for Blueberry Cake. Yields 12 servings.

HARD SAUCE FOR BLUEBERRY CAKE:
1 cup butter, softened
⅛ teaspoon salt

2 cups sifted powdered sugar
1 teaspoon vanilla or rum extract

Beat butter in a mixer bowl at high speed until creamy. Gradually add salt and powdered sugar, beating well after each addition. Beat until of sauce consistency, scraping bowl occasionally. Stir in vanilla. Chill, covered, 1 hour.

Note: May substitute 1 tablespoon cooking sherry for vanilla.

The Flavors of Mackinac (Michigan)

I always set my timer a few minutes less than the recipe calls for since it can always be baked more . . . but not less. To test whether a cake is ready to take out of the oven, first notice the sides are beginning to come away from the pan. A toothpick inserted in the center should come out clean or with just a few crumbs. You can also press your finger gently onto the cake, and it should leave none or a very slight impression. Slightly underbaking a cake is probably better than overbaking and ending up with a dry cake—but just right is just right!

Banana Nut Cake

This old-fashioned favorite is so easy to make. It is a deliciously moist cake, perfect for backyard picnics.

½ cup butter or margarine, softened
1 cup sugar
2 eggs
1 teaspoon vanilla
2 very ripe bananas, sliced

2¼ cups unbleached white flour
1¼ teaspoons baking soda
1 teaspoon salt
½ cup buttermilk
¾ cup coarsely chopped walnuts

Preheat oven to 350°. In a large mixing bowl, cream together butter and sugar. Beat in eggs and vanilla, mixing well. Add bananas, and beat again. On low speed, beat in flour, baking soda, and salt. Add buttermilk, and mix well; stir in walnuts.

Pour into a greased and floured 9x13-inch baking pan. Bake 30–35 minutes or until toothpick inserted in center of cake comes out clean. Remove from oven, and place on a wire rack to cool. Prepare Cream Cheese Frosting. When cool, frost cake. Serves 9–12.

CREAM CHEESE FROSTING:

3 ounces cream cheese, softened
2 tablespoons butter or margarine
1 teaspoon vanilla

1½ cups powdered sugar
1 tablespoon milk, as needed
¼ cup finely chopped toasted walnuts

In a medium bowl, mix together cream cheese, butter, and vanilla. Gradually beat in sugar until mixture is smooth and spreads easily. Add milk to thin, if necessary. Sprinkle with toasted walnuts.

San Juan Classics II Cookbook (Washington)

Sizes seem to change often. Cream cheese is hard to find in 3-ounce packages, so we are saying simply "3 ounces." You will need to cut ⅜ off the 8-ounce bar, which is a little less than half.

Banana Marshmallow Cake

During baking, marshmallows melt interestingly over the top of the cake.

2½ cups sugar
1 cup butter-flavored shortening
4 egg whites
3 cups all-purpose flour
1½ teaspoons baking powder
½ teaspoon salt
2 cups mashed bananas

6 tablespoons buttermilk or
   sour milk
1 teaspoon vanilla
¾ cup chopped nuts (optional)
¾ cup raisins (optional)
16 marshmallows

Cream sugar and shortening together in a large bowl. Add rest of ingredients except marshmallows, and mix thoroughly. Place marshmallows in a greased and floured 9x13-inch pan in rows 2 inches apart. Pour batter over the marshmallows. Smack pan smartly on counter until tops of marshmallows show through batter. Bake at 350° for 40–50 minutes till top is browned. Makes 18 pieces.

Recipes from Iowa with Love (Iowa)

Oatmeal Cake
with Broiled Coconut Topping

1½ cups boiling water
1 cup quick-cooking rolled oats
1½ cups sifted all-purpose flour
1 teaspoon baking soda
1 teaspoon salt
1 teaspoon ground cinnamon

½ teaspoon baking powder
½ cup butter or margarine, softened
1 cup sugar
1 cup firmly packed light brown
   sugar
2 large eggs

Preheat oven to 350°. Combine 1½ cups boiling water and oats; set aside. Sift together flour and next 4 ingredients. In a mixer bowl, beat butter and sugars at medium speed until mealy; add eggs, one at a time, beating until light and fluffy. Stir in oats; add flour mixture gradually, beating well. Pour batter into a greased and floured 9-inch square pan.

Bake at 350° for 40 minutes. Let cool in pan 10 minutes. Transfer cake to a baking sheet, and cool completely. Spread Coconut Topping over cake. Broil 2–3 minutes or until topping is lightly browned. Yields 8 servings.

COCONUT TOPPING:

1⅓ cups flaked coconut
¼ cup butter or margarine,
   melted

½ cup firmly packed brown sugar
¼ cup heavy cream or milk
1 teaspoon vanilla

Combine all ingredients in a bowl.

Lighthouse Secrets (Florida)

Lady Baltimore Cake

1 cup butter, softened
2 cups sugar
1 cup milk
3½ cups all-purpose flour

2 teaspoons baking powder
1 teaspoon vanilla
6 egg whites, stiffly beaten

Cream butter and sugar. Add milk, flour, baking powder, and vanilla, then fold in 6 beaten (soft peaks) egg whites. Bake at 350° in 3 greased 8- or 9-inch cake pans 20–25 minutes. Let cool.

FILLING:
2 egg whites
1½ cups powdered sugar
1 cup chopped raisins, soaked
   ten minutes in hot water

¾ cup sliced maraschino cherries
1 cup chopped nuts

Beat 2 egg whites until very stiff. Very gradually, add the powdered sugar, one tablespoon at a time. Fold in well-drained raisins and cherries; add nuts. Spread Filling between layers. Frost with Butter Icing.

BUTTER ICING:
½ stick butter, softened
2 cups powdered sugar

1 teaspoon vanilla
Milk

Cream butter, sugar and vanilla together; add just enough milk to make creamy and spreadable.

My Favorite Maryland Recipes (Maryland)

Add some cherry juice to the Butter Icing to give it a nice pink color as well as a hint of cherry flavor. Lady Baltimore would surely approve.

Lady Baltimore Cake

Wacky Cocoa Cake

3 cups unsifted all-purpose
  flour
2 cups sugar
½ cup cocoa
2 teaspoons baking soda
1 teaspoon salt
2 cups water
¾ cup vegetable oil
2 tablespoons vinegar
2 teaspoons vanilla extract

Combine flour, sugar, cocoa, baking soda, and salt in large mixer bowl. Add water, oil, vinegar, and vanilla; beat 3 minutes at medium speed until thoroughly blended. Pour batter into greased and floured 9x13-inch pan. Bake at 350° for 35–40 minutes or until cake tester inserted in center comes out clean. Cool; frost with Smooth 'n' Creamy Frosting.

SMOOTH 'N' CREAMY FROSTING:
2 (3-ounce) boxes pistachio
  instant pudding mix
¼ cup powdered sugar
1 cup cold milk
1 (8-ounce) tub Cool Whip,
  thawed

Combine pudding mix, sugar, and milk in a small bowl. Beat at lowest speed of electric mixer until well blended, about 1 minute. Fold in whipped topping. Spread on cake at once. Store cake in refrigerator.

Tried and True by Mothers of 2's (Ohio)

Pistachio nuts are indeed green, but the color of the gelatin product gets a little help to make it prettier. Kids seem to be magnetized to pistachio pudding and ice cream and fluff . . . and frosting! Over chocolate cake? Oh, yeah!

Three-Layer Italian Cream Cake

Doubling the frosting is recommended for this cake. It is so good, you will want to be sure to have plenty!

½ cup (1 stick) butter, softened
½ cup shortening
2 cups sugar
5 eggs, separated
2 cups all-purpose flour

1 teaspoon baking soda
1 cup buttermilk
1 teaspoon vanilla extract
1 (3-ounce) can flaked coconut
1 cup chopped pecans

Cream butter and shortening in mixing bowl until light and fluffy. Beat in sugar. Add egg yolks, and beat well. Whisk flour and baking soda together. Add to creamed mixture alternately with buttermilk, mixing well after each addition. Stir in vanilla, coconut, and pecans. Fold in beaten (soft peaks) egg whites. Pour into 3 greased and floured 8-inch cake pans. Bake at 350° for 25–30 minutes or until cake tests done. Cool in pan 10 minutes. Remove to a wire rack to cool completely.

FROSTING:

1 (8-ounce) package cream
   cheese, softened
¼ cup (½ stick) butter or
   margarine, softened

1 (1-pound) package powdered
   sugar
1 teaspoon vanilla extract
1 cup chopped pecans

Beat cream cheese and butter in mixing bowl until light and fluffy. Add powdered sugar, and mix well. Beat in vanilla. Spread Frosting between layers and over top and side of the cooled cake. Sprinkle top and side with pecans. Yields 10 servings.

Open House: A Culinary Tour (Tennessee)

Pecan Torte

Pecan lovers beware! This is to die for!

4 eggs, well beaten	1½ teaspoons baking powder
1 pound brown sugar	1 cup chopped pecans
1 cup all-purpose flour	1 teaspoon vanilla

Mix all ingredients, pour into 2 well-greased and floured 9-inch cake pans, and bake at 325° for 30–35 minutes. Cool completely before removing from pans. The layers will be thin.

FILLING:

1 tablespoon butter	5 teaspoons sugar
2 teaspoons all-purpose flour	1 cup chopped pecans
1 cup whipping cream, whipped	

Melt butter in top of double boiler. Blend in flour, stir in whipped cream, and cook until thick. Cool. Add sugar and nuts. Spread mixture between layers of torte. Serves 8–10.

ICING:

2 cups sweetened whipped cream	½ cup chopped pecans

Ice top and sides of torte with whipped cream, and sprinkle top with chopped nuts.

The Harvey Houses, Southeast Texas
Boardin' in the Thicket (Texas)

When hand-chopping is required, nuts are easier to chop after heating in the microwave on a paper plate on HIGH for two minutes, or in a baking pan in a 325° oven about five minutes. (Toasted nuts taste better, too.)

Georgia Pecan Cake

½ cup butter, softened
½ cup vegetable shortening
2 cups sugar
5 large eggs, separated
1 teaspoon vanilla

2 cups sifted all-purpose flour
1 teaspoon baking soda
1 cup buttermilk
1¼ cups chopped pecans
1¼ cups flaked coconut

Cream butter and shortening thoroughly. Gradually add sugar. Beat until fluffy. Add egg yolks and vanilla. Sift flour with baking soda 3 times. Add to batter alternately with buttermilk, beginning with flour and ending with flour. By hand, stir in nuts and coconut. Beat egg whites until stiff, but not dry. Carefully fold in all the egg whites. Bake at 350° in 3 greased large layer pans about 25 minutes or until done, or for about 1 hour in greased tube pan. Serves 12–16.

FROSTING:
1 (8-ounce) package cream
  cheese, softened
¾ stick butter, softened

1 (1-pound) box powdered sugar
1 teaspoon vanilla
½ cup chopped pecans

Mix together ingredients, and spread on cooled cake.

Grandma Mamie Jones' Family Favorites (Georgia)

Buttermilk is good to have on hand even if you don't like to drink it. Great for biscuits, cornbread, cakes, and of course, Mose's Buttermilk Pie (page 132).

The Best Carrot Cake Ever

The Best Carrot Cake Ever

And that's the truth!

2 cups sugar
1 cup vegetable oil
4 eggs
2 (4-ounce) jars strained baby
    food carrots
1 teaspoon vanilla

2 cups all-purpose flour
½ teaspoon salt
1½ teaspoons baking soda
2 teaspoons ground cinnamon
¼ teaspoon nutmeg
¼ teaspoon cloves

Combine sugar and oil; beat well. Add eggs, carrots, and vanilla; beat mixture until smooth. Combine remaining dry ingredients. Gradually add to creamed mixture, beating well. Pour batter into 2 greased and floured 9-inch round cake pans. Bake at 350° for 30 minutes or until a wooden toothpick comes out clean. Cool in pans for 10 minutes. Remove layers from pans. Cool completely on wire racks before icing. Serves 10–12.

CREAM CHEESE FROSTING:

1 (8-ounce) package cream
    cheese, softened
½ cup butter or margarine,
    softened

1 tablespoon vanilla
4 cups powdered sugar, sifted
1½ cups chopped pecans

Cream together cream cheese and butter. Add vanilla and powdered sugar, 1 cup at a time. Mix well and add pecans. Spread between layers and all over cake.

G.W. Carver Family Recipes (Virginia)

Chocolate Surprise Cupcakes

Don't be surprised at how fast these disappear.

3 cups all-purpose flour
2 cups sugar
½ cup cocoa
1 teaspoon salt
2 teaspoons baking soda

⅔ cup oil
2 cups water
2 tablespoons vinegar
2 teaspoons vanilla

Mix flour, sugar, cocoa, salt, and baking soda. Add oil, water, vinegar, and vanilla. Combine thoroughly; fill cupcake liners ⅔ full of mixture.

FILLING:
1 (8-ounce) package cream
    cheese, softened
1 egg

⅓ cup sugar
¼ teaspoon salt
1 cup chocolate chips

Mix cream cheese, egg, sugar, and salt until fluffy. Fold in chocolate chips. Drop one heaping teaspoon of Filling into muffin batter. Bake for 25 minutes at 350°. Frost, if desired.

Virginia City Alumni Association Cookbook (Nevada)

Filled Fudge Cake

If you like chocolate, you'll love this cake.

2 cups sugar
1 cup canola oil
1½ teaspoons salt
2 eggs
1 teaspoon vanilla
3 cups all-purpose flour

2 teaspoons baking powder
2 teaspoons baking soda
¾ cup unsweetened cocoa
1 cup buttermilk
1 cup hot water
1 cup chopped nuts (optional)

Cream sugar, oil, and salt. Add eggs and vanilla. Mix together flour, baking powder, baking soda, and cocoa. Add to creamed mixture alternately with buttermilk and hot water. Mix well. Add nuts, if desired. Grease a large Bundt or angel food cake pan. Pour ½ of batter into pan.

FILLING:

¼ cup sugar
1 teaspoon vanilla
1 (8-ounce) package cream
   cheese, softened

1 cup semisweet chocolate
   chips
½ cup flaked coconut (optional)

Mix all Filling ingredients together well, and drop by spoonfuls on top of first layer of cake batter. Then cover with remaining batter. Bake at 350° for 1 hour. Do not turn out of pan until completely cool (3–4 hours). Turn out onto plate. Ice with thin chocolate glaze, if desired.

The Pure Food Club of Jackson Hole (Wyoming)

Thin chocolate glaze? Mix 1½ cups powdered sugar, 2 teaspoons cocoa, and just a tad of milk to turn into a thin sauce.

My Chocolate Cake

My Chocolate Cake

Awesome cake! Best frosting there is! A treat to lick the bowl and beaters, that's for sure.

1 cup butter, softened	¾ cup cocoa
3 cups packed brown sugar	1 tablespoon baking soda
4 eggs	½ teaspoon salt
2 teaspoons vanilla	1½ cups sour cream
2⅔ cups all-purpose flour	1½ cups boiling water

In mixing bowl, beat butter and sugar; add eggs one at a time, beating well after each addition. Beat until light and fluffy. Blend in vanilla. Combine flour, cocoa, baking soda, and salt; add to creamed mixture alternately with sour cream, beating well after each addition. Stir in water until well blended. Pour into 3 greased and floured 9-inch round cake pans. Bake at 350° for 35 minutes.

FROSTING:

½ cup butter	5 cups powdered sugar
3 squares sweet chocolate	1 cup sour cream
3 squares semisweet chocolate	2 teaspoons vanilla

In saucepan, melt butter and chocolates over low heat. Cool. In mixing bowl, combine sugar, sour cream, and vanilla. Add chocolate mixture, and beat until smooth. Frost cooled cake. Makes 15 servings.

Montezuma Amish Mennonite Cookbook II (Georgia)

This recipe makes lots of delicious frosting, so you will easily have enough for 4 (8-inch) layers, which would raise this cake to even greater heights!

Century-Style Chocolate Sheet Cake

A tester could have sworn she was eating the cake from the Old Century Bar in downtown Dayton!

CAKE:

2 sticks butter
1 cup water
2 tablespoons cocoa
2 cups all-purpose flour
2 cups sugar

1 teaspoon baking soda
1 teaspoon salt
2 eggs, lightly beaten
½ cup buttermilk

Preheat oven to 375°. Combine butter, water, and cocoa in a large saucepan. Bring to a boil; immediately remove from heat. Stir in flour, sugar, baking soda, and salt. Mix thoroughly. Add eggs and buttermilk; stir. Pour into a greased jellyroll pan. Bake 20 minutes.

ICING:

1 stick butter
6 tablespoons milk
¼ cup cocoa
1 (1-pound) box powdered
    sugar

Pinch of salt
1 teaspoon vanilla
½–1 cup chopped pecans

Melt butter in a saucepan. Mix in milk, cocoa, powdered sugar, salt, and vanilla. Pour Icing over Cake while still hot. Spread Icing evenly, and sprinkle with pecans. Yields 20 servings.

Causing a Stir (Ohio)

Decadent Chocolate Cake

¾ cup butter, softened
2 cups sugar
2 eggs, separated
1 teaspoon vanilla
1 cup sour cream
1 teaspoon baking soda
1 (1⅓-ounce) package powdered
   whipped topping mix

2 cups all-purpose flour
¾ cup cocoa
1 teaspoon baking powder
1 (3-ounce) box chocolate fudge
   instant pudding mix
1¼ cups half-and-half

Cream butter and sugar; add egg yolks and vanilla. Beat one minute on high speed; set aside. Beat egg whites until soft peaks form; fold in sour cream; add baking soda and whipped topping mix. Add sour cream mixture to butter mixture. Mix flour, cocoa, baking powder, and pudding mix. Add alternately with half-and-half to butter mixture. Beat 2 minutes on high. Pour into 2 greased and lightly floured 8-inch pans. Bake at 350° for 35–40 minutes.

CREAMY CHOCOLATE FROSTING:
6 tablespoons butter, softened
¾ cup cocoa
3 cups powdered sugar

⅓ cup half-and-half
1 teaspoon vanilla

Cream butter; add cocoa and sugar alternately with half-and-half and vanilla. With electric mixer, beat until smooth. When cake is done, cool in pans for 10 minutes. Remove to wire rack to complete cooling. Frost.

Beyond Loaves and Fishes (New Mexico)

A pinch of baking soda seems to help prevent the frosting from cracking, and to keep it moist. A PINCH is all . . . don't get carried away.

Chips of Chocolate Peanut Butter Cake

Chips of Chocolate Peanut Butter Cake

Cut a slice to pack in your lunchbox for a special treat There's a taste of deliciousness in every single bite.

2¼ cups all-purpose flour	½ teaspoon baking soda
2 cups brown sugar	1 cup milk
1 cup peanut butter	1 teaspoon vanilla
½ cup margarine, softened	3 eggs
1 teaspoon baking powder	1 cup semisweet chocolate chips

In large bowl, blend first 4 ingredients at low speed until crumbly. Reserve 1 cup. Add remaining ingredients (except chocolate chips) to crumb mixture. Blend at low speed, then beat 3 minutes. Pour 2½ cups batter into greased Bundt pan. Sprinkle with chips and reserved crumb mixture. Spread remaining batter over this. Bake for 55–65 minutes at 350°. Cool completely.

GLAZE:

½ cup chocolate chips	2–3 tablespoons milk
1 tablespoon butter	½ cup powdered sugar

Combine first 3 ingredients in saucepan, and heat on low until melted. Beat in sugar. Drizzle on cake. Serves 16.

Country Cupboard (Wisconsin)

The sign of a good recipe is a repeat performance. Lest you forget which recipe you tried and liked, write a date and a comment in your cookbook above the recipe. And/or put a sticky note or tab on the page to easily get back to it. Serious cooks have a notebook or computer program with chapters like cakes, pies, etc., where you can list recipe title, book, and page number. Works for me.

Chocolate and Cherry Ring

This cake became a tradition to welcome home new moms and their babies in our neighborhood. It's a winner!

2 cups all-purpose flour	½ cup cooking oil
¾ cup sugar	2 teaspoons vanilla
1 teaspoon baking soda	1 (21-ounce) can cherry pie filling
1 teaspoon ground cinnamon	1 cup semisweet chocolate chips
⅛ teaspoon salt	1 cup chopped walnuts
2 eggs, beaten	Powdered sugar

In a large bowl, mix first 5 ingredients. In another bowl, combine eggs, oil, and vanilla; add to flour mixture. Mix well. Stir in cherry pie filling, chocolate chips, and walnuts. Turn into a 10-inch fluted well-greased Bundt pan. Bake at 350° for 1 hour. Cool on wire rack 15 minutes. Remove from pan. Cool. Sift powdered sugar on top, and serve. Serves 15.

Taste of Clarkston: Tried & True Recipes (Michigan)

Pineapple Zucchini Cake

3 eggs	2 teaspoons vanilla
2 cups sugar	1 (8¾-ounce) can crushed
1 cup oil	pineapple, drained
3 cups all-purpose flour	2 cups grated zucchini
1 teaspoon salt	1 cup chopped walnuts
1½ teaspoons cinnamon	1 cup white raisins, soaked in
4 teaspoons baking powder	1 cup boiling water, drained
1 teaspoon baking soda	

Cream eggs, sugar, and oil; sift flour, salt, cinnamon, baking powder, and soda; gradually add to mixture, and beat 2 minutes. Stir in vanilla, pineapple, and zucchini; add nuts and drained raisins. Spoon into greased and floured Bundt pan. Bake at 350° for 55–60 minutes. Pick-test with toothpick. Serves 15.

The Best of the Zucchini Recipes Cookbook (Pennsylvania)

Daffodil Cake with Lemon Sauce

With daffodils blooming right outside our windows and fresh blossoms on the cake plate, this has to be the most eye-catching cake we serve.

WHITE BATTER:

½ cup sifted cake flour
½ cup sifted powdered sugar
6 egg whites, at room
   temperature (save yolks)
½ teaspoon cream of tartar
½ teaspoon vanilla
⅛ teaspoon salt
½ cup sugar

Sift cake flour and powdered sugar together 6 times. Beat egg whites until frothy. Add cream of tartar, vanilla, and salt. Beat until soft peaks form. Gradually beat in sugar. Sift ¼ of the flour mixture at a time over egg mixture; fold in.

YELLOW BATTER:

¾ cup sifted cake flour
¾ teaspoon baking powder
6 egg yolks
2½ tablespoons lemon juice
1 tablespoon cold water
½ cup sugar
Powdered sugar

Sift cake flour and baking powder together 6 times. Beat egg yolks with lemon juice and water until thick, about 5 minutes. Gradually beat in sugar. Sift ¼ flour mixture at a time over egg mixture; fold in.

Alternately spoon Yellow and White Batters into an ungreased 9- or 10-inch tube pan. Bake at 375° for 35–40 minutes. Invert and cool. Dust with powdered sugar; serve with Lemon Sauce. Serves 14–16.

LEMON SAUCE:

½ cup sugar
1 tablespoon cornstarch
1 cup boiling water
½ cup fresh lemon juice
1 teaspoon lemon zest
2 tablespoons unsalted butter
Few grains of salt

In a medium saucepan, mix together sugar and cornstarch. Gradually add boiling water. Boil 5 minutes. Remove from heat, and add fresh lemon juice, zest, butter, and salt.

A Year of Teas at the Elmwood Inn (Kentucky)

Triple Lemon Ripple Cake

Triple Lemon Ripple Cake

Lemon lovers pucker up! This one's for you.

FILLING:

1 (8-ounce) package cream
   cheese, softened
⅓ cup sugar

1 egg
2 tablespoons all-purpose flour
2 tablespoons lemon juice

Beat cream cheese and sugar; beat in egg till fluffy. Add flour. Stir in lemon juice. Set aside.

BATTER:

½ cup butter, softened
1½ cups sugar
3 eggs
3 tablespoons lemon juice

2¼ cups all-purpose flour
2 teaspoons baking powder
½ teaspoon salt
½ cup milk

Preheat oven to 350°. Spray tube pan with cooking spray. Cream butter and sugar. Beat in eggs till mixture is very light and fluffy. Add lemon juice. Combine dry ingredients, and add to creamed mixture alternating with milk.

Pour ½ the Batter into pan. Cover with Filling, then pour in remaining Batter. Gently swirl knife through batter a few times. Bake 45–55 minutes until cake pulls away from sides of pan. Cool in pan 10 minutes. Turn out and cool completely.

GLAZE:

2 tablespoons lemon juice   1½ cups powdered sugar

Stir lemon juice into powdered sugar. Drizzle over cake. Makes 10–12 servings.

Still Cookin' After 70 Years (Nevada)

True lemon lovers can add extra lemon zest to Filling, Batter, and Glaze. Lemonylicious!

Lemon Buttermilk Cake

3 cups all-purpose flour
½ teaspoon salt
½ teaspoon baking soda
½ teaspoon baking powder
2 cups sugar

1 cup vegetable oil
4 eggs
1 cup buttermilk
2 tablespoons lemon extract

Preheat oven to 325°. Measure flour, sift, then re-measure. Re-sift flour with salt, baking soda, and baking powder. With electric mixer on low speed, beat sugar, oil, eggs, buttermilk, and extract until just blended. Slowly add flour mixture to egg mixture while blending, then beat on medium speed 4 minutes. Bake about 1 hour in greased and floured tube pan.

When cake is done, gently loosen edges of cake while hot. While still in pan, pour Glaze over cake, then return to oven for 3 minutes. Remove and allow to cool in pan. Serves 15.

GLAZE:
2½ cups powdered sugar,
   sifted
5 tablespoons lemon juice

3 tablespoons orange juice
2 tablespoons orange marmalade
½ teaspoon salt

Combine ingredients well. Pour over hot cake in pan.

Sandlapper Cooks (South Carolina)

Flour measures differently after sifting. If you measure two cups, then sift it and measure again, you'll have some left over. So pay attention to how it's worded: two cups flour is more than two cups sifted flour. My mother always sifted, measured, then poked a table knife all the way to the bottom of the measuring cup to settle the flour; then she put a little more on top and leveled it off again. That's the biggest reason her famous Grammy Cookies were always crispy.

Eggnog Pound Cake

Eggnog is not in the ingredients, but the taste has a hint of the otherwise indescribable flavor. Delicious and moist . . . with a crusty top.

2 sticks butter, softened (1 cup)
½ cup shortening
3 cups sugar
5 large eggs
1 teaspoon vanilla extract
1 teaspoon coconut extract
1 teaspoon almond extract
1 teaspoon butternut extract
1 teaspoon lemon extract
1 teaspoon rum extract
3 cups cake flour
1 cup evaporated milk

Cream butter, shortening, and sugar. Add eggs, one at a time, beating well after each. Add extracts, one at a time, mixing thoroughly after each addition. Alternately add flour and milk, beginning and ending with flour. Pour into a greased and floured 10-inch tube pan. Bake at 300° for 1 hour and 45 minutes. Serves 15.

Sand in My Shoes (Florida)

Ever Moist Coconut Pound Cake

2 sticks butter, softened
½ cup shortening
3 cups sugar
5 eggs
3 cups all-purpose flour

½ teaspoon salt
1 teaspoon baking powder
1 cup milk
2 teaspoons coconut flavoring
1 (7-ounce) bag coconut flakes

Beat butter and shortening together; add sugar, and beat until mixed. Add eggs one at a time; beat until fluffy. Mix dry ingredients together, and add alternately with milk, ending with flour mixture; beat well. Add flavoring and coconut. Pour into greased 10-inch tube pan, and bake at 350° for 75 minutes, or until straw comes out clean. Serves 15.

SYRUP TOPPING:

⅔ cup sugar
⅓ cup water

1 teaspoon coconut flavoring
2 teaspoons butter

Boil sugar, water, flavoring, and butter for 1 minute. Immediately pour boiling syrup onto cake upon removing from oven. Let sit 10 minutes before removing from pan. Wrap cake with plastic wrap while still hot.

Tangier Island Girl (Virginia)

Hawaiian Sunset Cake

Hawaiian Sunset Cake

Yum! Yum! Yum!

1 (18¼-ounce) box orange
    supreme cake mix
1 (3-ounce) box vanilla instant
    pudding mix

1 (3-ounce) box orange gelatin
4 eggs
½ cup oil
1½ cups milk

Mix all ingredients together. Beat 3 minutes on medium speed. Pour into 3 greased and floured 9-inch cake pans. Bake in 350° oven 30 minutes. Cool layers.

FILLING:

1 (20-ounce) can crushed
    pineapple, drained well
1 (12-ounce) package frozen
    flaked coconut

1 (8-ounce) container sour
    cream
2 cups sugar

Mix all ingredients. Reserve 1 cup mixture for Topping. Spread Filling between layers and on top of cake.

TOPPING:

1 (8-ounce) container frozen
    Cool Whip, thawed

1 cup Filling mixture

Mix together. Spread Topping on side and top of cake (over Filling, which is already on top of cake). Store in refrigerator. Serves 8–10.

The Best of Mayberry (North Carolina)

Grate a little orange peel on top for extra orangy flavor . . . and appeal. Orange slices are the perfect decoration. This is a beauty.

Pineapple-Orange Sunshine Cake

Talk about crowning glory—this frosting is spectacular.

1 (18¼-ounce) box yellow cake mix	4 eggs
½ cup oil	1 (11-ounce) can Mandarin orange sections (undrained)

Combine cake mix, oil, eggs, and oranges; mix at medium speed in electric mixer until almost smooth. Spoon into 2 greased and floured 8-inch cake pans. Bake at 325° for 25 minutes or until done. Cool cake in pans 10 minutes; remove from pans, and cool completely on racks. When very cool, split both layers. Spread frosting between layers, on top, and on side of cake. Store in refrigerator. Serves 8–10.

PINEAPPLE CHEESECAKE FROSTING:

1 (20-ounce) can crushed pineapple, undrained	1 tablespoon sugar
1 (10½-ounce) box cheesecake filling mix	1 (8-ounce) carton sour cream
	1 (8-ounce) container Cool Whip, thawed

Combine pineapple, cheesecake filling mix, sugar, and sour cream. Stir until mixture thickens. Fold in Cool Whip, mixing thoroughly.

Family Favorites (Louisiana)

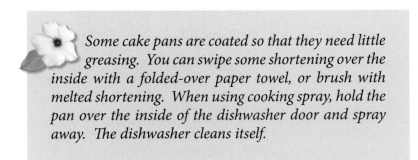

Some cake pans are coated so that they need little greasing. You can swipe some shortening over the inside with a folded-over paper towel, or brush with melted shortening. When using cooking spray, hold the pan over the inside of the dishwasher door and spray away. The dishwasher cleans itself.

Tearoom Lemon Cake

Easy, beautiful, and delicious!

1 (18¼-ounce) box yellow
   cake mix
½ cup butter, softened
6 eggs
½ cup heavy cream
½ cup water

1 tablespoon lemon zest
1 teaspoon vanilla
¾ cup seedless raspberry preserves,
   divided
1½ cups sliced almonds, toasted

Preheat oven to 350°. Grease 2 (9-inch) springform pans with 2¾-inch sides. Combine cake mix, butter, eggs, cream, water, lemon zest, and vanilla. Beat about 2 minutes, or until smooth. Divide batter between prepared pans. Bake 25–30 minutes or until a toothpick inserted in the center comes out clean. Cool thoroughly on racks. After cooling, cut around side of pans to loosen; release sides, and remove cakes. Cut each cake in half horizontally, resulting in 4 layers.

Place one layer, cut side up, on a cake plate. Spread with ¼ cup preserves, then ¾ cup Lemon Frosting. Repeat layers twice. Top with final cake layer, cut side down. Frost sides and top with remaining Lemon Frosting. Press almonds into sides of cake, and chill at least 2 hours or until frosting sets. Serves 10–15.

LEMON FROSTING:

3 (8-ounce) packages cream
   cheese, softened
1 (11¾-ounce) jar lemon curd

1 cup powdered sugar
3 tablespoons fresh lemon juice
1 tablespoon lemon zest

Cream together ingredients until smooth.

Faithfully Charleston (South Carolina)

This can be done in four (9-inch) cake pans, and you won't have to split them. Careful to smooth batter to achieve even layers, and check for doneness after twenty minutes.

Apricot Cream Cheesecake

FILLING:

2 (8-ounce) packages cream
  cheese, softened
1 cup Angel Flake coconut

½ cup sugar
2 tablespoons lemon juice

Mix together cream cheese, coconut, sugar, and lemon juice. Let sit while making Batter.

BATTER:

1 (18¼-ounce) box Duncan
  Hines Butter Cake Mix
½ stick butter or margarine,
  softened

1 tablespoon lemon extract
3 eggs, beaten
¾ cup apricot nectar

Combine cake mix, butter, lemon extract, eggs, and nectar. Beat well. Pour into well-greased and floured Bundt or tube cake pan. Spoon Filling on Batter, being careful not to touch sides of pan or the tube. Bake in preheated 350° oven for 1 hour. Remove, and let stand in pan for 1 hour. During this time, make Glaze. Serves 15.

GLAZE:

2 cups powdered sugar
2 tablespoons lemon juice

2 tablespoons apricot nectar
1 tablespoon lemon extract

Mix ingredients together. Reverse pan onto cake plate; remove, and glaze top with Glaze; let it drip down the sides.

The Cookbook AAUW (New York)

Strawberry Cake

Make this cake one day in advance so it gets good and gooey!

1 (18¼-ounce) box white
  cake mix
1 (3-ounce) box strawberry
  gelatin

½ cup vegetable oil
1 cup chopped strawberries
4 eggs

In a large mixing bowl, combine cake mix and gelatin. Add oil and strawberries. Add eggs one at a time, beating well after each addition. Pour batter into greased 9x13-inch baking pan. Bake at 350° for 30–35 minutes. Serves 9–12.

GLAZE:
1 (1-pound) box powdered sugar   ¾ cup chopped strawberries
1 stick butter, melted

Combine Glaze ingredients, and spoon over cooled cake.

Sharing Our Best–Franklin (Tennessee)

Editor's Extra: You can use frozen strawberries, measuring a little less than fresh, but we prefer chopped, fresh strawberries in the Glaze.

Aunt Lottie's Banana Nut Cake

This cake does better in the refrigerator, but can travel well for a couple of hours in a cool vehicle. It cuts beautifully and has always been well received.

1 (18¼-ounce) box yellow cake mix

Prepare cake mix according to package directions in 3 greased 9-inch pans. Let cool.

FILLING:

3 medium to large ripe bananas, mashed
⅓ cup water
½ cup sugar
2 egg yolks, slightly beaten

Cook bananas, water, sugar, and egg yolks over medium heat in heavy saucepan until mixture thickens, stirring constantly, 8–10 minutes. Set this aside to cool. This mixture will thicken more as it cools.

7-MINUTE FROSTING:

1½ cups firmly packed light brown sugar
1 teaspoon vanilla
¼ cup water
2 egg whites, unbeaten
6–8 tablespoons chopped pecans, divided

Combine all ingredients except pecans in top of double boiler; beat on high speed of hand mixer over boiling water for a full 7 minutes, scraping sides of pot well upon completion.

Place first layer of cake on cake plate; spread ⅓ of the banana mixture to within ½ inch of the edge (this is important). Spread a heaping spoon of Frosting over Filling, completely covering bananas; sprinkle 2 tablespoons pecans over Frosting, and repeat with other 2 layers. Frost side of cake with remaining Frosting, adding more to the top if you have extra. Sprinkle entire top with more chopped pecans. Serves 10–12.

Let's Say Grace Cookbook (Alabama)

Banana Split Cake

1 (18¼-ounce) box banana
  cake mix
2 cups Cool Whip, thawed,
  divided
1 (8¾-ounce) can crushed
  pineapple, well drained

1 cup sliced fresh strawberries
1 (11- to 12-ounce) container
  fudge ice cream topping
½ cup chopped peanuts
Bananas for garnish
Lemon juice

Prepare cake mix according to package directions. Bake in 2 (8-inch) greased cake pans. Set aside to cool.

Fold pineapple into half of Cool Whip, and strawberries into other half. Heat and stir fudge topping until warm (not hot). Split cake layers in half. Place one layer on plate, and cover with strawberry mixture. Place another cake layer on top, and cover with half of fudge mixture, and half of peanuts. Place another cake layer on top of peanuts, and cover with pineapple mixture. Place last cake layer on top, and cover with remaining fudge and peanuts. Garnish with banana slices that have been dipped in lemon juice. Store in refrigerator.

Heavenly Helpings (West Virginia)

Pumpkin Pie Cake

1 (29-ounce) can pumpkin
1 (12-ounce) can evaporated
  milk
3 eggs, beaten
1¼ cups sugar
2 teaspoons cinnamon
1 teaspoon nutmeg

½ teaspoon salt
½ teaspoon ginger
½ teaspoon cloves
1 (18¼-ounce) box yellow
  cake mix
1 cup chopped walnuts
1 cup butter, melted

Combine all ingredients except cake mix, nuts, and butter. Pour into greased 9x13-inch pan. Sprinkle dry cake mix over pumpkin mixture. Pat down gently with spoon. Sprinkle with chopped nuts. Drizzle melted butter over cake. Bake 50–60 minutes in 350° oven.

Favorite Island Cookery Book III (Hawaii)

Orange Blooms

Too wonderful to eat just one.

1 (18¼-ounce) box yellow
 cake mix
4 eggs
¾ cup orange juice

1 (3-ounce) box instant lemon
 pudding mix
¾ cup oil

Mix all ingredients, and pour into mini muffin pans sprayed with non-stick cooking spray. Bake in preheated 350° oven for 8–10 minutes.

GLAZE:
2 tablespoons oil
2 cups powdered sugar

⅓ cup plus 2 tablespoons
 orange juice

Mix all ingredients until smooth. Dip top of cooled cupcakes in Glaze, and set on wire rack. Makes 48 cupcakes.

A Southern Collection: Then and Now (Georgia)

Wet and Wild Coconut Cake

1 (18¼-ounce) box yellow cake
 mix without pudding
1 (15-ounce) can Coco Lopez
 (cream of coconut)
1 (14-ounce) can Eagle Brand
 condensed milk

1 (7-ounce) bag flaked coconut
1 (16-ounce) container Cool
 Whip

Bake cake in a greased 9x13-inch pan according to directions on box.
    When cake is almost cooled, poke holes with fork all over the cake. Combine Coco Lopez and condensed milk. Stir until blended. Slowly spoon mixture over cake. Cover with plastic wrap, and refrigerate. Mix coconut and Cool Whip together. Store in a separate container in refrigerator. Ice the cake just before serving. Serves 9.

At the End of the Fork (Georgia)

Ugly Duckling Pudding Cake

1 (18¼-ounce) box yellow
   cake mix
1 (3-ounce) box lemon instant
   pudding mix
1 (16-ounce) can fruit cocktail,
   including syrup

1 cup flaked coconut
4 eggs
¼ cup oil
½ cup firmly packed brown
   sugar
½ cup chopped nuts (optional)

Blend all ingredients except brown sugar and nuts in large mixer bowl. Beat 4 minutes at medium speed of electric mixer. Pour into greased and floured 9x13-inch pan. Sprinkle with brown sugar and nuts. Bake at 325° for 45 minutes or until cake springs back when lightly pressed and pulls away from sides of pan. Do not underbake. Cool in pan 15 minutes. Spoon hot Butter Glaze over warm cake. Serve warm or cool, with prepared whipped topping, if desired. Serves 12.

BUTTER GLAZE:
½ cup butter or margarine
½ cup sugar

½ cup evaporated milk
1½ cups flaked coconut

Combine butter, sugar, and milk in saucepan; boil 2 minutes. Stir in coconut.

90th Anniversary Trinity Lutheran Church Cookbook (Kansas)

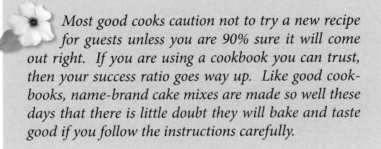

Most good cooks caution not to try a new recipe for guests unless you are 90% sure it will come out right. If you are using a cookbook you can trust, then your success ratio goes way up. Like good cookbooks, name-brand cake mixes are made so well these days that there is little doubt they will bake and taste good if you follow the instructions carefully.

Mother's Easter Cake

1 (18¼-ounce) box yellow
  cake mix
1 (20-ounce) can crushed
  pineapple, in juice
¾ cup sugar

2 (3-ounce) boxes vanilla instant
  pudding mix
3 cups milk
1 cup Dream Whip or Cool Whip
1 cup flaked coconut, toasted

Bake cake in greased 9x13-inch pan according to directions. When cake is done, prick with fork at 1-inch intervals. Combine pineapple with juice and sugar. Cook over medium heat until thick and syrupy. Stir occasionally. Pour pineapple mixture over cake, and spread evenly. Cool completely.

Combine pudding mix with milk; blend until thick. Spread over cake. Spread prepared Dream Whip or Cool Whip over cake. Refrigerate for 24 hours. Before serving, sprinkle with toasted coconut. Serves 12.

Heavenly Helpings (West Virginia)

Church Social Cake

½ tablespoon butter
2 (21-ounce) cans country apple
  filling
1 (18¼-ounce) box spice cake
  mix

½ cup flaked coconut
1½ cups quick oatmeal
1 cup chopped walnuts or pecans
⅓ cup sugar
2 sticks butter, melted

Grease a 9x13-inch baking dish with ½ tablespoon butter. Pour apple filling into dish and spread evenly. Spread cake mix over apple filling to an even thickness. Spread coconut and oats over cake mix to an even thickness. Sprinkle chopped nuts and sugar over entire mixture. Pour melted butter over entire cake, and bake at 375° for 50–60 minutes or until done. Serves 12.

Favorite Recipes Home-Style (Tennessee)

Carrot Pudding Cake

1 (18¼-ounce) box yellow cake mix	¼ cup oil
1 (3-ounce) box vanilla instant pudding mix	3 cups grated carrots
	½ cup finely chopped raisins
4 eggs	½ cup chopped walnuts
⅓ cup water	½ teaspoon salt
	2 teaspoons ground cinnamon

Blend all ingredients in large mixing bowl; beat 4 minutes with electric mixer on medium speed. Pour into 2 greased and floured 5x9-inch loaf pans. Bake at 350° for 40–50 minutes, until cakes spring back when lightly pressed and begin to pull away from sides of pans. Do not underbake. Cool in pans 15 minutes; remove, and cool on racks. Frost with Orange Cream Cheese Frosting. Serves 18.

ORANGE CREAM CHEESE FROSTING:

1 tablespoon butter or margarine, softened	1 teaspoon grated orange rind
	1 tablespoon orange juice
3 ounces cream cheese, softened	2½ cups sifted powdered sugar

Blend butter, cream cheese, and orange rind until smooth. Alternately add powdered sugar and orange juice, beating after each addition until smooth.

Calling All Cooks (Alabama)

Swiss Chocolate Cake

For those who like more frosting than cake, this is it! Light and luscious.

1 (18¼-ounce) box Swiss
   chocolate cake mix
2 eggs
1 cup oil

1½ cups buttermilk
1 (3-ounce) box vanilla instant
   pudding mix

Mix all together with mixer until smooth, and pour into 3 greased 9-inch round cake pans. Bake per instructions on cake mix box. Serves 8–10.

FILLING:

1½ cups powdered sugar
¾ cup sugar
11 ounces cream cheese,
   softened

1 (16-ounce) and 1 (8-ounce)
   carton Cool Whip
1 (1½-ounce) regular-size Hershey's
   candy bar

Mix sugars and cream cheese in mixer. Add Cool Whip. Spread one inch of frosting between layers. Frost top and outside. Grate Hershey's bar on top.

A Collection of My Favorite Recipes (Mississippi)

If you are not confident in dividing cake batter into pans, use an ice cream scoop to get more even layers.

Swiss Chocolate Cake

Self-Filling Chocolate Chip Cupcakes

1 (18¼-ounce) box chocolate or yellow cake mix

Make cake according to package directions. Spoon batter into 24 greased or paper-lined muffin tins, filling ⅔ full.

FILLING:

1 (8-ounce) package cream cheese, softened
1 egg, slightly beaten

⅓ cup sugar
1 cup semisweet chocolate chips

In mixing bowl, beat cream cheese, egg, and sugar until smooth. Fold in chips. Drop by tablespoonfuls into batter. Bake at 350° for 20 minutes or until tests done. Allow to sit for at least 10 minutes before removing from muffin tin.

From Our Home to Yours (North Carolina)

Chocolate Chip Bundt Cake

1 (18¼-ounce) yellow cake mix
3 eggs
¾ cup Wesson oil
1 (3½-ounce) box chocolate instant pudding mix (large box if you prefer)

¾ cup water
1 tablespoon vanilla
1 (8-ounce) carton sour cream
1 (12-ounce) bag semisweet chocolate chips

Mix all ingredients, except chocolate chips, with mixer until blended. Stir in chocolate chips. Pour into greased and floured Bundt pan and bake at 325° for 60 minutes. Serves 16.

Food for the Flock Volume II (Tennessee)

Butterfingers Cake

Talk about a guilty pleasure! This one takes "the cake."

1 (18¼-ounce) box yellow
    cake mix
1 (14-ounce) can condensed milk
1 (12-ounce) jar caramel topping

8 (2-ounce) regular-size
    Butterfinger candy bars,
    crushed, divided
1 (16-ounce) container Cool Whip

Bake cake in a 9x13-inch pan according to directions on box. Mix condensed milk and caramel topping. While cake is still hot, poke holes in top, and pour caramel mixture over cake so that the liquid seeps through the holes. Sprinkle crumbs from 6 of the candy bars on top, and let cool. Cover with plastic wrap, and refrigerate until cold. Frost with Cool Whip. Sprinkle remaining candy crumbs on top. Serves 12.

Treasured Favorites (Alabama)

Kahlúa Cake

1 (18¼-ounce) box chocolate
   cake mix
1 (3-ounce) box chocolate
   instant pudding mix

½ cup Crisco oil
4 eggs
¾ cup cooled strong coffee
¾ cup Kahlúa

Mix all ingredients together, and beat 4 minutes at medium speed. Bake in greased and floured Bundt pan at 350° for 40–45 minutes.

KAHLÚA FROSTING:
½ stick butter or margarine,
   softened
2 (1-ounce) packages Nestle
   unsweetened chocolate,
   melted

1 (1-pound) box powdered sugar
2 tablespoons strong coffee
3 tablespoons Kahlúa

Cream butter and chocolate. Add powdered sugar while continuing to beat. Add coffee and Kahlúa. Spread on cooled cake. Serves 16.

Recipes from the Heart (South Carolina)

Diane's Heath Cake

1 (18¼-ounce) box German
   chocolate cake mix
1 (12-ounce) jar caramel
   ice cream topping

1 (14-ounce) can condensed milk
1 (8-ounce) carton Cool Whip
3 regular-size Heath candy bars,
   crushed

Bake a 9x13-inch cake according to directions on package. When cake is done, right out of oven, poke holes all over cake with fork. Heat ice cream topping and condensed milk, and mix well. Pour over warm cake. When cake is cooled completely, top with Cool Whip. Sprinkle with crushed Heath bars. Store in refrigerator. Serves 12–15.

Fishin' for a Cure (Kentucky)

Praline Cake

This elevates pralines to new heights. Whoa!

1 (18¼-ounce) box yellow cake mix, prepared according to directions

Pour cake batter into 2 greased and floured 9x13x2-inch pans. Bake at 350° for about 20 minutes, or until cake leaves sides of pan. Remove from oven, and cool.

PRALINE TOPPING:

1 (1-pound) package light
  brown sugar
2 tablespoons all-purpose flour
2 eggs, beaten

½ cup butter, melted
1 teaspoon vanilla
1½ cups coarsely chopped
  pecans

In skillet, mix light brown sugar, flour, and eggs in melted butter, and cook for 3 minutes over low heat. Remove from heat, and stir in vanilla and pecans. Spread evenly over surface of cooled cakes. Bake 8 minutes at 400° to set the topping. Cool, and cut into 1½-inch strips. Makes 60 bite-size servings.

Pirate's Pantry (Louisiana)

Praline Brownies

Extra moist and chewy. We defy anyone to guess that these scrumptious brownies come from a mix. Must do ahead.

1 (22½-ounce) box brownie mix
¾ cup firmly packed light
   brown sugar

3 tablespoons margarine, melted
¾ cup chopped pecans

Prepare brownie mix according to package directions; do not add nuts. Place in greased 9x13x2-inch pan. In small mixing bowl, combine remaining ingredients. Sprinkle over brownie batter. Bake at 350° for 25–30 minutes. Cut when thoroughly cooled. These freeze well or can be stored in a tin. Makes 2 dozen.

Perennials (Georgia)

Pecan Pie Surprise Bars

1 (18¼-ounce) box Pillsbury
   Plus yellow or butter cake
   mix, divided
⅓ cup butter or margarine,
   softened

4 eggs, divided
1½ cups dark corn syrup
½ cup firmly packed brown sugar
1 teaspoon vanilla
1 cup chopped pecans

Heat oven to 350°. Grease 9x13-inch pan. Reserve ⅔ cup of dry cake mix for filling. In large bowl, combine remaining dry cake mix, butter, and 1 egg at low speed until well blended. Press in bottom of greased pan. Bake at 350° for 15–20 minutes or until light golden brown. In large bowl, combine reserved ⅔ cup dry cake mix, corn syrup, brown sugar, vanilla, and remaining 3 eggs at low speed until moistened. Beat one minute at medium speed or until well blended. Pour filling mixture over warm base. Sprinkle with pecans. Bake an additional 30–35 minutes or until filling is set. Cool completely. Cut into bars. Store in refrigerator. Makes 36 bars.

What's Cookin' in Melon Country (Colorado)

Caramel Bars

1 (18¼-ounce) box butter pecan
   cake mix
½ cup margarine, softened
1 egg

1 (12½-ounce) jar caramel
   topping
⅓ cup chopped nuts
⅓ cup flaked coconut

In large mixing bowl, stir together cake mix, margarine, and egg. Press half of mixture in bottom of 9x13-inch pan. Bake at 350° for 10 minutes. Pour caramel topping over baked crust. Sprinkle with nuts and coconut. Spread remaining half of cake mixture on top. Bake at 350° for 20–25 minutes or until lightly browned. Cool thoroughly. Cut into bars. Yields 24 bars.

Irene's Country Cooking (Wyoming)

Caramel Layer Choco-Squares

1 (14-ounce) package caramels
⅔ cup evaporated milk,
   divided
1 (18¼-ounce) box German
   chocolate cake mix

⅔ cup softened butter
½ cup chopped nuts
1 (12-ounce) package chocolate
   chips

In a heavy saucepan, melt unwrapped caramels in ⅓ cup of milk over low heat; set aside. In a large bowl, combine cake mix, butter, and nuts. Mix until dough is crumbly, but holds together. Press ½ the dough into a greased and floured 9x13-inch pan. Bake at 350° for 6 minutes. Remove from oven. Sprinkle chocolate chips over dough. Pour caramel mixture over chips. Top with remaining dough. Bake for 15–20 minutes. Chill. Makes 2 dozen.

Nutbread and Nostalgia (Indiana)

Nell's Apricot Bars

1 (18¼-ounce) box Duncan
　Hines Yellow Butter Recipe
　Cake Mix (do not substitute)
1 cup all-purpose flour
1½ sticks margarine, softened
1 cup chopped pecans
1 cup flaked coconut
1 (10- to 12-ounce) jar apricot
　preserves

Combine cake mix and flour. Cut margarine into cake mix mixture. Add nuts and coconut. Mix well. Pat ⅓ mixture into a 9x13-inch ungreased pan. Spread apricot preserves over mixture. Crumble remaining mixture over preserves. Bake 1 hour at 325°.

Gingerbread . . . and all the trimmings (Texas)

Pumpkin Sumpthin'

1 cup milk
3 eggs
1 cup sugar
1 teaspoon cinnamon
¼ teaspoon ginger
⅛ teaspoon cloves
½ teaspoon salt
1 (29-ounce) can pumpkin
1 (18¼-ounce) box yellow cake mix
1½ sticks margarine, melted
¾ cup chopped nuts
Whipped cream

Combine milk, eggs, sugar, spices, salt, and pumpkin; mix well. Pour into greased 9x13-inch baking pan. Sprinkle dry cake mix over top of mixture. Drizzle melted margarine over top. Sprinkle nuts over top. Bake at 350° for 1 hour or until browned. Serve with whipped cream. Serves 12.

Church Family Recipes (Nevada)

Cheesecakes

Snickers Cheesecake

Snickers Cheesecake

1½ cups graham cracker crumbs
2 cups sugar, divided
¼ cup butter, melted
4 (8-ounce) packages cream
    cheese, softened
1 tablespoon vanilla
Pinch of salt

4 large eggs, room temperature
16 fun-size Snickers bars, divided
4 tablespoons milk, divided
2 cups plus 2 tablespoons sour
    cream, divided
Whipped cream for garnish

Stir together graham crackers and ¼ cup sugar in bowl. Drizzle in butter, and stir well with fork. Press evenly into 10-inch springform pan.

Beat cream cheese and 1½ cups sugar at medium speed until softened and fluffy. Add vanilla and salt, and blend. Add eggs one at a time on lowest speed. Pour over crust.

Chop 10 candy bars. Combine with 2 tablespoons milk. Cook and stir over very low heat until smooth. Spoon over cheesecake batter in parallel stripes. With a knife, cut across the strips to swirl melted candy into batter. Bake at 350° for 1 hour or until done. Edges should be firm and center should move slightly. Cool 10 minutes.

Chop remaining 6 candy bars, and melt with remaining 2 tablespoons milk over low heat. Beat together with 2 cups sour cream and remaining ¼ cup sugar. Spread sour cream mixture over cheesecake. Bake at 350° for 10 minutes. Remove from oven, and drizzle remaining 2 tablespoons sour cream in a decorative pattern. Return to oven for 3 minutes. Refrigerate immediately. May serve with whipped cream and whole or sliced candy bars for decoration. Serves 12–15.

50 Years and Still Cookin'! (Ohio)

Cut a tiny hole in the corner of a plastic sandwich bag to drizzle decorative sour cream, or just spread over top circle of cake, as we did here.

Pat's Arizona Chocolate Turtle Cheesecake

3 cups chocolate cookie crumbs
5 tablespoons melted butter or
   margarine
1 (14-ounce) package caramels
   (approximately 50)
5 ounces evaporated milk
½ cup chopped, toasted pecans
2 (8-ounce) packages cream
   cheese, softened

½ cup sugar
1 teaspoon vanilla
2 large eggs
½ cup semisweet chocolate pieces,
   melted
Whipped cream (optional)

Combine crumbs and butter. Press into side and bottom of 9-inch springform pan. Bake 10 minutes at 350°.

In heavy pan, melt unwrapped caramels with milk over low heat. Stir frequently until smooth. It takes a while. (They scorch easily; don't get on the phone.) Pour over crust, and top with nuts.

Combine cream cheese, sugar, and vanilla. Mix at medium speed on electric mixer until well blended. Add eggs, one at a time, mixing well. Blend in chocolate. Pour over nut-topped crust. Bake 40 minutes at 350°. When done, the top will crack gently at the outside edge. Take it out of the oven. Do not overbake. Loosen cake from rim of pan. Cool before removing rim. Chill. Garnish with whipped cream, if desired. Serves 10–12.

Outdoor Cooking (Arizona)

> *Be aware that fat-free cream cheese doesn't work the same in cheesecakes. It is made with skim milk and the texture is not as creamy as regular cream cheese. Low-fat, or Neufchatel cheese, is softer, (doesn't need to be softened for mixing), and is almost interchangeable with regular. It will work fine for all the cheesecakes in this book.*

Irish Cream Cheesecake

This will be a WOW!!! dessert at your next party.

CRUST:

2 cups Oreo cookie crumbs　　**6 tablespoons butter, melted**
¼ cup sugar

Preheat oven to 350°. Combine Oreo crumbs and sugar in bowl; add melted butter. Mix well, and press into bottom of a 9-inch springform pan. Bake 7–10 minutes.

FILLING:

4 (8-ounce) packages cream　　**1½ cups Irish cream liqueur**
　cheese, softened　　　　　　**1 tablespoon vanilla**
1⅔ cups sugar　　　　　　　　**1 cup semisweet chocolate chips**
5 eggs

Beat cream cheese until smooth; add sugar and eggs, beating until fluffy. Add liqueur and vanilla; mix well. Sprinkle chocolate chips over Crust. Spoon Filling over chips. Bake for 1 hour and 20 minutes, or until center is set. Cool completely in pan.

TOPPING:

1 cup whipping cream　　　　**½ cup semisweet chocolate chips,**
2 tablespoons sugar　　　　　　**melted**

Beat cream and sugar in a large, chilled bowl until stiff. Continue to beat while adding melted chocolate. Spread mixture over cheesecake.

CHOCOLATE CURLS:
2 cups semisweet chocolate chips

Melt chocolate in a small saucepan over low heat. Pour onto a baking sheet. Let stand at room temperature until set, but not firm. To make curls, pull a thin knife or cheese plane across surface of chocolate (curls will break if chocolate is too firm). Re-melt and cool as necessary to form desired number of curls. Arrange on cake. Refrigerate until ready to serve. Serves 16 or more.

A Pinch of Rose & A Cup of Charm (Mississippi)

Fantasy Chocolate Cheesecake

A delicious decadent dessert!

CHOCOLATE CRUMB CRUST:

1⅓ cups Oreo cookie crumbs
1 tablespoon sugar

4 tablespoons (½ stick) butter, at
    room temperature

Mix cookie crumbs with sugar and butter. Pat in an even layer over bottom of a 9-inch springform pan.

CHEESECAKE:

¼ cup Kahlúa
1½ cups semisweet chocolate
    chips
2 tablespoons butter
2 eggs
⅓ cup sugar

¼ teaspoon salt
1 cup (½ pint) sour cream
2 (8-ounce) packages cream
    cheese, room temperature
½ cup sour cream, for topping

Put Kahlúa, chocolate chips, and butter in small saucepan over low heat. Stir constantly until chocolate melts and mixture is smooth; set aside to cool slightly. Heat oven to 325°. Beat eggs in small bowl. Beat in sugar, salt, and sour cream. Drop small pieces of cream cheese into egg mixture, continuing to beat until smooth. Gradually beat in chocolate mixture. Pour into springform pan over crust. Bake until filling is just barely set in center, about 40 minutes.

Take pan out of oven and let stand at room temperature 1 hour. Spread on ½ cup sour cream; refrigerate cheesecake several hours.

KAHLÚA CHOCOLATE SAUCE:

1 cup semisweet chocolate chips
⅓ cup Kahlúa

⅓ cup light corn syrup

Heat chocolate chips with Kahlúa and corn syrup over low heat until chocolate melts and mixture is smooth.

Unhinge pan and cut cold cheesecake in small slices with thin, sharp knife dipped in cold water. Dip knife before each cut, and wipe clean between cuts. Pour a bit of sauce over top of each slice. Yields 12 servings.

Jan Townsend Going Home (California)

Fantasy Chocolate Cheesecake

Amaretto Cheesecake

CRUST:

1½ cups chocolate wafer
   cookie crumbs
½ cup finely chopped toasted
   almonds

¼ cup butter, melted
2 tablespoons sugar
1 tablespoon amaretto

Place rack in middle of oven. Preheat oven to 375°. Grease a 9-inch springform pan.

Mix all ingredients together in large bowl till well blended. Press into bottom of springform pan; bake till brown, about 7 minutes, but no longer than 9 minutes. Cool on a rack. Decrease oven temperature to 350°.

FILLING:

3 (8-ounce) packages cream
   cheese, at room temperature
1 cup sugar
4 eggs

⅓ cup whipping cream
⅓ cup finely chopped almonds
¼ cup Bailey's Irish Cream
¼ cup amaretto

Using an electric mixer, slowly beat cream cheese and sugar till light and fluffy. Add eggs, one at a time, beating well after each addition. Add remaining ingredients for Filling, and beat till well blended. Pour Filling into Crust. Bake until just set, about 1 hour. Turn off oven, and let cheesecake cool inside oven with oven door open, approximately 30 minutes. Center of cheesecake should be completely set by this time. Remove cake from pan. Preheat oven again to 350°.

TOPPING:

1½ cups sour cream
1 tablespoon sugar

½ teaspoon vanilla

Blend ingredients in small bowl till smooth. Spread this mixture over cake. Bake 10 minutes. Cover with plastic wrap; refrigerate overnight. Serves 10–12.

Home at/on the Range with Wyoming BILS (Wyoming)

Easy Brandy Alexander Cheesecakes

CAKES:

½ cup butter, softened
2 (8-ounce) packages cream
   cheese, softened
2 eggs
¾ cup sugar
¼ cup all-purpose flour

2 teaspoons crème de cocoa or
   Kahlúa
2 teaspoons brandy
1 cup whipping cream
15 chocolate sandwich cookies
   (Oreos)

Cream butter and cream cheese. Beat in eggs. Add sugar, flour, crème de cocoa, brandy, and whipping cream. Beat until well mixed. Line cupcake tins with 30 paper liners. Twist cookies apart and place half in each of the liners (filling side up). Fill with batter until almost full. Bake at 350° for 25–30 minutes or until lightly browned; cool.

TOPPING:

1 cup whipping cream
¼–½ teaspoon instant coffee
   powder
1 teaspoon brandy

1 teaspoon crème de cocoa or
   Kahlúa
2 teaspoons sugar
Freshly grated nutmeg for garnish

Combine all Topping ingredients. Stir, and store in refrigerator for 10 minutes or longer. Remove from refrigerator, and beat until soft peaks form. Frost the cheesecakes with this mixture, and sprinkle with nutmeg. Store in refrigerator.

Cardinal Country Cooking (Wisconsin)

Blueberry Swirl Cheesecake

Blueberry Swirl Cheesecake

This is the easiest cheesecake I have ever found. It tastes like a traditional recipe, but it's not as time-consuming. You don't need a springform pan for this cheesecake, and the swirls of fruit make this beautiful as well as delicious.

2 (8-ounce) packages cream
   cheese, softened
½ cup sugar
¼ teaspoon vanilla

2 eggs, beaten
1 graham cracker crust
1 (21-ounce) can blueberry
   pie filling, divided

Beat cream cheese, sugar, and vanilla until smooth. Add eggs, and mix. Pour into crust. Drop several tablespoonfuls of pie filling onto top of cream cheese mixture (about ½ the can). Swirl blueberries with a knife. Bake at 350° for 35–40 minutes. Cool on wire rack. Chill for at least 2 hours. Serve with remaining blueberry pie filling. Serves 8–10.

Gritslickers (North Carolina)

Almond Cheesecake
with Raspberries

1¼ cups graham cracker crumbs
⅓ cup butter, melted
¼ cup sugar
2 (8-ounce) packages cream
   cheese, softened
1 (16-ounce) can ready-to-spread
   vanilla frosting

1 tablespoon lemon juice
1 tablespoon grated lemon peel
3 cups Cool Whip
Raspberries and sliced almonds
   for garnish

Stir together crumbs, butter, and sugar in a small bowl; press onto bottom and ½ inch up side of a 9-inch springform pan or pie plate. Chill. Beat cream cheese, frosting, lemon juice, and peel in a large mixing bowl at medium speed with electric mixer until well blended. Fold in whipped topping; pour over crust. Chill until firm. Arrange raspberries and almonds on top. Serves 12.

Sandy Hook Volunteer Fire Co. Ladies Aux. Cookbook (Connecticut)

Cranberry-Swirl Cheesecake

CRANBERRY PURÉE:

4 cups cranberries
1 cup water

1 cup sugar

Combine cranberries, water, and sugar in a saucepan, and bring to a boil. Simmer until the berries pop, about 15 minutes. Allow to cool, then purée in a food processor or blender. You can strain the purée when it is hot, but be careful when you process it—hot liquids explode out of blenders. Strain out skins and seeds, then chill. This sauce keeps well for up to 1 week, refrigerated. Makes 2 cups.

CHEESECAKE:

4 (8-ounce) packages cream
   cheese, softened
1¾ cups sugar

4 large eggs
4 tablespoons Cranberry Purée,
   divided

Cream together cream cheese and sugar, scraping the bowl well. There should be no lumps. Add eggs 1 at a time, scraping the bowl between additions. Pour ⅓ of the batter evenly into a buttered and lined 8x3-inch baking pan and drizzle 2 tablespoons of the Cranberry Purée over the top. Pour another ⅓ of the batter over the purée, trying not to disturb the pattern, then drizzle 2 more tablespoons Cranberry Purée over the top. Pour in the remaining batter, smoothing carefully.

Place Cheesecake in another pan containing enough water to come halfway up the sides of the cheesecake pan. If you are using a spring-form pan, be sure to wrap it in foil so the water doesn't seep in. Bake in a preheated 350° oven until set in center, about 1½ hours.

Cool completely, then turn out onto a serving platter, and refrigerate. The Cheesecake freezes well at this point. To serve, thaw to refrigerated temperature before glazing.

(continued)

(Cranberry-Swirl Cheesecake continued)

GLAZE:

**4 ounces Callebaut semisweet
  chocolate**
¼ cup water

¼ cup Cranberry Purée
**Whipped cream and cranberries
  for garnish**

Melt chocolate and water in microwave, or on stovetop over low heat. Whisk in ¼ cup Cranberry Purée until the mixture is smooth and shiny. Allow to cool until thick enough to coat Cheesecake. Pour Glaze over Cheesecake, creating a thick layer. Smooth top with flat knife, allowing large, even dribbles to decorate sides of Cheesecake.

To serve, thin remaining Cranberry Purée with a little water until you have a sauce. Pool some sauce on each plate and top with a piece of Cheesecake. Garnish with cranberries and lightly sweetened whipped cream rosettes. Holly leaves make a nice garnish for the winter holiday season. Pass remaining sauce around in a small pitcher. Makes 1 (8-inch) Cheesecake.

The Shoalwater's Finest Dinners (Washington)

Fresh cranberries are hard to find except in season, which is in the fall. But they freeze very well. Don't wash, just place the bag in a freezer bag, and they can last for up to a year; use just like you would fresh—no need to thaw. If thawed, berries will be soft; it is easier to chop or grind them while frozen. Lesson here, if you like fresh cranberry dishes, buy extra when they are in season.

White Chocolate Raspberry Cheesecake Santacafé

Make this when you want to have twenty slices of sheer pleasure to impress your guests. This Raspberry Sauce freezes beautifully and looks elegant drizzled over the cheesecake.

CRUST:

2 cups graham cracker crumbs
1 cup slivered blanched almonds

¼ cup clarified butter in its
    liquid (unchilled) form

In food processor, blend graham cracker crumbs and almonds until almonds are ground fine; add butter, and combine well. Press onto bottom and ⅔ of the way up side of 10-inch springform pan.

FILLING:

8 ounces fine quality white
    chocolate (Callebaut)
4 (8-ounce) packages cream
    cheese, softened
½ cup plus 2 tablespoons sugar

4 large whole eggs
2 large egg yolks
2 tablespoons all-purpose flour
1 teaspoon vanilla
2 pints raspberries

In metal bowl set over pan of barely simmering water, melt chocolate, stirring until smooth; remove bowl from heat.

In large bowl with an electric mixer, beat cream cheese until light and fluffy. Add sugar, and beat in whole eggs and egg yolks, one at a time, beating well after each addition. Beat in flour and vanilla. Add melted chocolate in a slow stream, beating until combined well.

Scatter raspberries over the bottom of crust; pour filling over, and bake in middle of a preheated 350° oven for 1 hour, or until top is firm to the touch. Let cool in the pan on a rack; chill, covered loosely overnight, then remove side of pan. Serves 12.

(continued)

Even if you don't clarify the butter, it is perfectly delicious!

(White Chocolate Raspberry Cheesecake Santacafé continued)

RASPBERRY SAUCE:

2 (12-ounce) packages frozen raspberries in syrup, thawed

¼ cup sugar

3 tablespoons Grand Marnier liqueur

Use syrup from 1 package of raspberries; drain the other. Combine all ingredients in food processor or blender; strain to remove seeds. Chill until ready to use. Drizzle over plate; place cheesecake slice on top.

Note: Butter is made up of butterfat, milk solids, and water. Clarified butter is the translucent golden-yellow butterfat left over after the milk solids and water are removed. You can do this yourself by melting butter over low heat and skimming off the milk solids and water, which look like foam, leaving just the clear, golden butterfat.

Recipes from Our House (Colorado)

Italian Swirl Cheesecake

This cheesecake keeps well in refrigerator and also freezes well.

CHOCOLATE NUT CRUST:

¾ cup chocolate wafer crumbs (10 wafers)
¾ cup finely chopped almonds
2 tablespoons sugar
3 tablespoons melted butter

Preheat oven to 350°. Mix chocolate wafer crumbs, nuts, and sugar together. Put in bottom of 9-inch springform pan. Pour melted butter over top, use a fork to blend mixture, and press into bottom of pan. Cook 15–20 minutes until lightly browned. Remove, and cool slightly. Reduce oven to 325°.

CHEESECAKE:

2 (8-ounce) packages cream cheese, softened
1 cup sugar, divided
2 tablespoons all-purpose flour
2 tablespoons vanilla
6 eggs, separated
1 cup sour cream
3 ounces semisweet chocolate
2 tablespoons amaretto

In food processor or with electric mixer, beat cream cheese until soft. Beat in ¾ cup sugar, flour, and vanilla. Mix until well blended. Beat in egg yolks and sour cream. In a separate bowl, beat egg whites and remaining ¼ cup sugar until soft peaks form. Fold egg whites into cream cheese mixture. Pour ⅔ of batter into baked crust. Melt chocolate with amaretto in top of double boiler. Add to remaining batter. Gently blend. Starting at outside edge, pour chocolate batter onto white batter in a swirl pattern, ending up in middle of pan.

Place in 325° oven for 50 minutes. Turn the oven off. Prop door open 2–3 inches and let cheesecake sit for 2 hours. Remove to rack to cool. Chill before serving. I usually serve this with chocolate sauce. Serves 10–12.

The Old Yacht Club Inn Cookbook (California)

Cookies

Mom-Mom's Sugar Cookie Cutouts with Glaze

Mom-Mom's Sugar Cookie Cutouts with Glaze

At Mom-Mom's on Christmas Eve, there was homemade fudge, cakes, and cookies of all sorts, especially her frosted cut-out cookies—those were everybody's favorite. Everybody was happy. There was Christmas music playing; the tree was all decorated and the lights were on; everything was perfect.

COOKIES:

2 cups sifted all-purpose flour	¾ cup sugar
1 teaspoon cream of tartar	½ cup oil
½ teaspoon baking soda	2 eggs
½ teaspoon salt	1 teaspoon vanilla

Sift flour, cream of tartar, baking soda, and salt into a bowl. In another bowl, add sugar, oil, and eggs; beat until smooth. Add vanilla; mix thoroughly. Gradually add flour mixture to sugar mixture, beating after each addition. Chill dough until it can be easily handled, 3–4 hours.

Grease cookie sheets. Heat oven to 375°. Roll dough out, ½ at a time, on lightly floured table top to ¼-inch thickness. Use cutters to make cookies; dip cutters into flour to keep them from sticking. Place onto cookie sheets and bake at 375° for 10–12 minutes. Put on racks to cool. Frost with Glaze when cool. Makes 1½–2 dozen cookies.

GLAZE:

¾ cup powdered sugar	3–4 teaspoons milk

Mix powdered sugar and milk until smooth and of frosting consistency, adding a few more drops of milk, if needed. Glaze hardens as it stands.

You may want to add different colors of food coloring to each ¾ cup Glaze that you make.

Editor's Extra: If dough gets soft and sticky while cutting into shapes, chill, then rework.

Mom-Mom's Cookbook (West Virginia)

Biscotti Italian Cookies

This recipe is an old Milanese recipe.

1 cup shortening or margarine,
   softened
3 eggs
5 cups all-purpose flour
½ teaspoon salt (optional)
1 cup sugar

⅓ cup milk
1 teaspoon vanilla extract
4 teaspoons baking powder
1 (12-ounce) package mini
   chocolate chips
Powdered sugar for garnish

Mix all ingredients. Knead a little. Make into 2-inch, finger-shaped cookies, and place on ungreased baking sheet. Bake at 350° for 10–12 minutes or until light brown. When cool, sprinkle with powdered sugar.

St. Ambrose "On the Hill" Cookbook (Missouri)

Almond Butter Cookies

This is the best recipe I have ever found for cut-out cookies. They are soft, not crispy. Be sure your icing is not too runny, and let the cookies get thoroughly cool before decorating.

1 cup butter, softened
1 (8-ounce) package cream
   cheese, softened
1½ cups sugar
1 egg

1 teaspoon vanilla
½ teaspoon almond extract
3½ cups all-purpose flour
1 teaspoon baking powder
Milk and powdered sugar icing

Mix butter, cream cheese, and sugar until fluffy. Add egg, vanilla, and almond extract. Stir together flour and baking powder; add to creamed mixture and mix thoroughly. Roll out to ¼-inch thickness, and cut into shapes. Bake at 350° for 8–10 minutes. Don't overbake. Ice cooled cookies with a little milk and powdered sugar combined.

Welcome Home (Alaska)

Old-Fashioned Sour Cream Cookies

½ cup soft shortening
1½ cups sugar
2 eggs
1 cup thick sour cream
1 teaspoon vanilla

2¾ cups all-purpose flour, sifted
½ teaspoon baking soda
½ teaspoon baking powder
½ teaspoon salt

Preheat oven to 425°. Mix together shortening, sugar, and eggs. Stir in sour cream and vanilla. Sift dry ingredients together, and stir into other mixture. Chill at least 1 hour.

Drop rounded teaspoonfuls about 2 inches apart onto lightly greased baking sheet. Bake 8–10 minutes, until lightly browned, and when touched with finger, almost no imprint remains. Frost with Butter Icing when cool.

BUTTER ICING:

3 cups powdered sugar, sifted
¼ cup butter, softened or melted

About 3 tablespoons cream
1½ teaspoons vanilla

Combine ingredients until smooth.

Ohio State Grange (Blue) Cookbook (Ohio)

There are two clues that this is an old recipe. Did you find them? They are "soft" and "thick"—no need for those adjectives today. All bought vegetable shortening stays soft enough to mix right out of the container. And, unlike homemade that goes through stages, all bought sour cream is "thick."

Apricot Lilies

A butter cookie that blossoms with taste.

¼ cup sugar
1 cup unsalted butter, softened
3 ounces cream cheese, softened
1 teaspoon vanilla
2 cups all-purpose flour

¼ teaspoon salt
Approximately ½ cup apricot jam
   (or another fruit jam)
Powdered sugar for garnish

Combine sugar, butter, cream cheese, and vanilla. Beat at medium speed until well mixed, about one minute. Reduce speed to low; add flour and salt. Continue beating until well mixed, 1½–2 minutes. Divide dough into 4 parts. Wrap each in plastic food wrap. Refrigerate until firm, at least 2 hours.

On lightly floured surface, roll out ¼ of the dough at a time to ⅛-inch thickness. Keep remaining dough refrigerated. Cut with 2-inch round cookie cutter. Place on cookie sheets ½ inch apart. Spoon a small amount of jam onto each cookie. With thin spatula, fold dough over jam to form a lily shape. Gently press narrow end to seal. Jam will show on top of cone-shaped cookie.

Heat oven to 375°. Bake 7–11 minutes, or until edges are lightly browned. Cool completely. Sprinkle lightly with powdered sugar. Makes approximately 8 dozen cookies.

St. Mary's Family Cookbook (Wisconsin)

It's important to use butter, stick margarine (with at least 80% oil), or shortening to make successful cookies. Reduced-fat products contain air and water, and will yield tough, flat, underbrowned cookies.

Vienna Crescents

This Christmas cookie is an all-time favorite any time of the year.

½ cup sugar
1 cup butter, softened
2 cups all-purpose flour, sifted
1¼ cups ground almonds

1 teaspoon vanilla
¼ teaspoon salt
Powdered sugar for garnish

Cream sugar and butter until fluffy. Add flour, ¼ cup at a time. Add almonds, vanilla, and salt. Shape dough into balls, and wrap in wax paper. Refrigerate for one hour.

Take off 1-inch pieces of chilled dough, and roll on flat surface into a strip 1 inch wide and ½ inch thick. Shape into a crescent. Bake on lightly greased cookie sheets at 350° for 15–20 minutes. Cool on sheets a bit, then transfer to cooling racks. When completely cooled, dust with powdered sugar. Makes 4 dozen.

Good Things to Eat (New Jersey)

Ginger Crinkles

Their aroma spreads throughout the inn when baking, so we often bake them just before serving on chilly afternoons. They go deliciously with apple cider in the autumn.

¾ cup margarine, softened
1 cup brown sugar
1 egg
½ cup molasses
2½ cups all-purpose flour
2 teaspoons baking soda

1 teaspoon cinnamon
½ teaspoon cloves
2 teaspoons powdered ginger
½ teaspoon salt
Sugar for coating cookies

Cream margarine and sugar. Add egg, and beat well. Mix in remaining ingredients. Chill dough. Form into small balls, and roll in sugar. Sprinkle each ball with 2 or 3 drops of water to create crinkled effect. Bake at 375° for 12 minutes. Cool slightly before removing from cookie sheets. Makes about 48 cookies.

The Queen Victoria® Cookbook (New Jersey)

Lemon Bon Bons

1 cup butter, softened
⅓ cup powdered sugar
¾ cup cornstarch

1¼ cups sifted self-rising flour
½ cup finely chopped
pecans

Preheat oven to 350°. Cream butter and sugar until light and fluffy. Add cornstarch and flour, and mix well. Refrigerate overnight.

Shape dough into ¾-inch balls; place on wax paper that has been scattered with nuts. Use bottom of glass (dipped in flour) to flatten balls to ¼ inch thick. Using spatula, place on ungreased cookie sheet, nut side up. Bake 6–8 minutes at 350°. Cool and frost.

LEMON FROSTING:
1 cup powdered sugar
1 tablespoon butter, softened

1 tablespoon lemon juice
Food coloring

Blend sugar, butter, and lemon juice until smooth. Divide and color. Swirl on top of cookie. Yields 2–3 dozen.

Cookin' to Beat the Band (Indiana)

Cherry and Sesame Cookies

2 sticks (1 cup) butter, softened
¼ cup sugar
1 teaspoon almond extract
2 cups all-purpose flour
¼ teaspoon salt
Sesame seeds
⅓ cup halved candied cherries

In a mixing bowl, cream butter and sugar until light and fluffy. Add almond extract, flour, and salt. Beat until just mixed. Refrigerate to chill. Shape into 1-inch balls, roll in sesame seeds, press a cherry half on top, and bake on greased cookie sheets in preheated 400° oven for about 10 minutes. Let them sit in the oven for another 2–3 minutes, then put them on a rack to cool. Makes 3 dozen.

The Black Hat Chef Cookbook (Pennsylvania)

Mom's Toasted Oatmeal Cookies

1 cup sugar
½ cup brown sugar
2 eggs
2 teaspoons vanilla
½ cup Crisco shortening (very
    important, do not substitute)
½ cup margarine
1 cup oatmeal, toasted in oven
    at 350° for 5 minutes
1 teaspoon baking soda
1 teaspoon salt
2 cups plus 4 tablespoons
    all-purpose flour
½ cup chopped nuts
1 cup chocolate chips, raisins,
    or craisins (dried cranberries)

Cream first 6 ingredients together. Stir in dry ingredients, nuts, and chocolate chips. Drop by teaspoon onto cookie sheet, and flatten with a glass dipped in sugar. Bake at 350° for 8 minutes. Makes about 40.

Cooking at Thimbleberry Inn (Wisconsin)

Chocolate Lace Cookies

1 cup oatmeal (6-minute or
   quick variety)
1 cup sugar
¼ teaspoon baking powder
2 tablespoons plus 2 teaspoons
   all-purpose flour

1 tablespoon plus 1 teaspoon cocoa
¼ pound butter or margarine,
   melted
1 egg, beaten
1 teaspoon vanilla

Mix dry ingredients; add melted butter, egg, and vanilla. Drop by tea-spoon onto wax paper on cookie sheet, 4 inches apart. Bake at 300° for 6–8 minutes. Cool on wax paper for 15 minutes. Peel cookie from paper. Dough can be made ahead and frozen. Makes 3½ dozen (3-inch) cookies.

The Philadelphia Orchestra Cookbook (Pennsylvania)

Sticky Toffee Tea Cookies

This toffee cookie is flat and airy, similar to a lace cookie.

¾ cup all-purpose flour
¾ cup old-fashioned oatmeal
½ teaspoon salt
½ teaspoon baking soda
7 (1-ounce) English toffee
  candy bars, coarsely chopped

6 tablespoons light brown sugar
6 tablespoons sugar
1½ teaspoons vanilla
1 egg
5 tablespoons butter, softened
5 tablespoons solid shortening

Preheat oven to 325°. In a medium bowl, combine flour, oatmeal, salt, and baking soda. Add chopped candy, and set aside.

In a large mixing bowl, mix brown sugar, sugar, vanilla, and egg. Add butter and shortening, and mix well. Add candy/flour mixture, and blend well. Drop by tablespoonfuls one inch apart on lightly greased cookie sheet. Bake 8–10 minutes or until golden. Remove from oven, and cool on wire rack. Makes about 36.

The Tea Table (Kentucky)

Chippy Peanut Butter Cookies

3 sticks butter, softened
1½ cups peanut butter
1½ cups sugar
1½ cups brown sugar
3 eggs, beaten
1 teaspoon vanilla extract

3¾ cups all-purpose flour
2¼ teaspoons baking soda
1½ teaspoons baking powder
¾ teaspoon salt
3 cups peanut butter chips
3 cups butterscotch chips

Cream together butter, peanut butter, and both sugars until smooth. Beat in eggs and vanilla. Sift together flour, baking soda, baking powder, and salt. Stir into creamed mixture; blend well. Stir in peanut butter and butterscotch chips. Refrigerate 30 minutes.

Preheat oven to 350°. Shape dough into 1-inch balls, and arrange on ungreased cookie sheets, 2 inches apart. Press down on each cookie with the tines of a fork. Bake 10–12 minutes (10 for chewy, 12 for crispy). Cooling on cookie sheet will let them firm up. Makes 100 or more.

Our Daily Bread, and then some . . . (New York)

Opie's Trick or Treat Cookies

The best trick is to treat yourself to these.

½ cup butter or margarine,
    softened
1 cup sugar
1 cup plus 2 tablespoons firmly
    packed brown sugar
3 eggs
2 cups peanut butter

¾ teaspoon light corn syrup
¼ teaspoon vanilla extract
4½ cups regular oats, uncooked
2 teaspoons baking soda
¼ teaspoon salt
1 cup M&M candies
6 ounces semisweet chocolate chips

Cream butter; gradually add sugars. Beat well with an electric mixer at medium speed. Add eggs, peanut butter, syrup, and vanilla. Beat well. Add oats, baking soda, and salt; stir well. Stir in remaining ingredients (dough will be stiff). Pack dough into a ¼-cup measure. Drop dough, 4 inches apart, onto lightly greased cookie sheets. Lightly press each cookie into a 3½-inch circle with fingertips. Bake at 350° for 12–15 minutes (centers of cookies will be slightly soft). Cool slightly on cookie sheets; remove to wire racks and cool completely. Makes 2½ dozen.

Aunt Bee's Delightful Desserts (North Carolina)

Chocolate Waffle Cookies

1½ cups sugar
1 cup shortening (or ½
    margarine and ½ shortening)
4 eggs
2 tablespoons vanilla

2 cups all-purpose flour
½ cup cocoa
¼ teaspoon salt
1 (16-ounce) can chocolate
    frosting

Blend sugar, shortening, and eggs well. Add vanilla, and stir in flour, cocoa, and salt. Drop by spoonfuls onto hot waffle iron, close, and bake one minute. While still warm, frost with chocolate frosting.

Heavenly Delights (Nebraska)

Cappuccino Flats

2½ cups chocolate chips, divided
½ cup plus 3 tablespoons
   shortening, divided
6 tablespoons butter, softened
¼ cup brown sugar
¼ cup sugar

1 tablespoon instant coffee
1 teaspoon water
1 egg
2 cups all-purpose flour
1 teaspoon cinnamon
¼ teaspoon salt

Melt 1 cup chocolate chips on HIGH in microwave 1 minute or more; stir till smooth. While that cools slightly, beat ½ cup shortening and butter until soft. Add brown sugar and sugar, and beat until fluffy. Stir coffee crystals into water until dissolved. Add coffee mixture, melted chocolate, and egg to butter mixture, and beat well. Mix in flour, cinnamon, and salt. Cover, and chill about 1 hour.

Shape into 2 (7-inch) rolls. Wrap, and chill overnight.

Cut into ¼-inch slices, and bake on ungreased sheet in 350° oven for 10–12 minutes. Cool on racks.

Melt 1½ cups chocolate chips and 3 tablespoons shortening in microwave, stirring occasionally. Dip ½ of each cookie into chocolate mixture. Place on racks until set. Makes about 55 cookies.

Sharing Our Best (Alaska)

Editor's Extra: Use white and/or dark chocolate bark for thicker coating.

Chocolate-Covered Cherry Cookies

Chocolate-Covered Cherry Cookies

COOKIE DOUGH:

½ cup butter, softened
1 cup sugar
1 egg
1½ teaspoons vanilla
1½ cups all-purpose flour

½ cup cocoa
¼ teaspoon salt
¼ teaspoon baking soda
24–48 maraschino cherries,
    drained, reserve juice

Cream butter, sugar, egg, and vanilla. Add remaining ingredients, except cherries. Blend. Dough will be stiff. Shape dough into 48 (1-inch) balls. Place balls 2 inches apart on ungreased cookie sheet (or spray with nonstick spray). Push ½ (or whole) cherry into each ball. When all cookies are molded, prepare Chocolate Frosting and use immediately.

CHOCOLATE FROSTING:

1 cup semisweet chocolate chips
½ cup sweetened condensed
    milk

¼ teaspoon salt
1½ teaspoons reserved cherry
    juice

Melt chocolate with milk, stirring constantly. Remove from heat. Add remaining ingredients. Stir until smooth. Spread ½ teaspoon Frosting over each cherry. Bake at 350° for 8–10 minutes. Yields 4 dozen cookies.

Recipes from the Heart (Nevada)

This is a very pretty cookie whose frosting is thick, so actually stays where you spread it. I like to leave a bit of the cherry showing to tempt with the ruby treasure inside.

The Best of All
Chocolate Chip Cookies

1 cup solid shortening
½ cup butter or margarine,
    softened
1⅓ cups sugar
1 cup brown sugar
4 eggs
1 tablespoon vanilla
1 teaspoon lemon juice

2 teaspoons baking soda
1½ teaspoons salt
1 teaspoon cinnamon
½ cup rolled oats
3 cups all-purpose flour
2 (12-ounce) packages semisweet
    chocolate chips
2 cups chopped walnuts

In large bowl, beat shortening, butter, and sugars until light and fluffy, about 5 minutes. Add eggs, one at a time, beating well after each addition. Beat in vanilla and lemon juice.

In another bowl, stir together baking soda, salt, cinnamon, oats, and flour. Beat into creamed mixture until well combined; stir in chocolate chips and nuts.

For each cookie, drop a scant ¼ cup dough onto a lightly greased baking sheet, spacing cookies about 3 inches apart. Bake in a 350° oven for 16–18 minutes or until golden brown. Transfer to racks, and let cool. Makes about 3 dozen large cookies.

A Century of Mormon Cookery, Volume 1 (Utah)

The Richest Lunch Box Cookies Ever

Gourmet cookies have become a staple. Start making these for friends and neighbors, and you may find yourself becoming the new Mrs. Fields or David. These lunch box gems make wonderful gifts, too—just fill a tin for birthdays, Christmas gifts, or last-day-on-the-job parties.

2 (3½-ounce) bars caramel-filled Swiss chocolate, such as Lindt
2 ounces bittersweet or semisweet chocolate
2 ounces white chocolate
1 cup pecan halves
1½ cups regular oatmeal, divided (not quick-cooking)
1 cup butter, softened
1½ cups lightly packed brown sugar
½ teaspoon salt
2 teaspoons vanilla
2 eggs
1½ cups all-purpose flour
½ teaspoon baking powder
½ teaspoon baking soda

Preheat oven to 350°. Break caramel bars at natural sections. Cut sections into small chunks with a sharp knife. (You may chill bars first if you like—it helps to keep caramel from oozing out too much as you cut them.) Set chunks aside. Grate bittersweet or semisweet chocolate and white chocolate.

Chop pecans. Place ½ cup oatmeal in blender, and blend at high speed until oatmeal turns to powder. In a large bowl, beat butter with sugar, salt, and vanilla until creamy. Add eggs, and beat well. Stir in the flour, powdered oatmeal, remaining oatmeal, baking powder, and baking soda. Add caramel chunks, both grated chocolates, and pecans, and mix just to combine.

Using 2 spoons or your hands, form balls the size of large walnuts. Place them in rows about 3 inches apart on ungreased cookie sheets. Bake for 10–15 minutes until golden brown. Remove cookies from sheet, and cool on a rack. When cool, store cookies in an airtight container. Yields about 4 dozen cookies.

J. Bildner & Sons Cookbook (Massachusetts)

Cocoa Mint Wafers

1½ cups all-purpose flour
¾ cup unsweetened cocoa
1¼ teaspoons baking powder
¼ teaspoon salt
¾ cup butter or margarine,
  softened

1¼ cups sugar
1 large egg
24 rectangular mint wafers (such
  as Andes)

Mix flour, cocoa, baking powder, and salt; set aside. In a large bowl, beat butter and sugar with electric mixer until fluffy. Beat in egg, and with mixer on low, gradually add flour mixture until blended. Divide dough in half. Shape each half into a 9-inch long roll. Wrap in wax paper, and refrigerate about 4 hours, until very firm.

Heat oven to 375°. Lightly grease cookie sheets, or line with parchment paper. Cut each roll into 24–32 slices. Place 1 inch apart on cookie sheets. Bake 10–12 minutes, until cookies look dry. Remove to a wire rack to cool completely.

In a small saucepan, melt mints over low heat. Cool slightly, then put in a zipper-type plastic sandwich bag. Snip off a tiny corner and drizzle chocolate over cooled cookies. Refrigerate 15 minutes for chocolate to harden.

Dutch Pantry Simply Sweets (West Virginia)

Instead of a bowl, put dry ingredients onto a sheet of wax paper, or an inexpensive bendable paper plate. Now you can pour ingredients easily into mixer bowl—and no extra bowl to clean up!

Cocoa Mint Wafers

Death-By-Chocolate Cookies

Even more decadent when served with ice cream!

2 (8-ounce) packages semisweet
    chocolate, or candy coating,
    divided
¼ cup firmly packed brown
    sugar
¼ cup butter or margarine

2 eggs, beaten
1 teaspoon vanilla
½ cup all-purpose flour
¼ teaspoon baking powder
2 cups chopped pecans

Heat oven to 350°. Coarsely chop half the chocolate; set aside. Microwave remaining 8 squares chocolate in large bowl on HIGH 1–2 minutes. Stir until chocolate is melted and smooth. Stir in sugar, butter,
eggs, and vanilla. Stir in flour and baking powder. Stir in reserved
chopped chocolate and nuts. Drop by ¼ cupfuls onto a parchment-
lined or greased cookie sheet. Bake 10–12 minutes, until cookies rise
and are set to the touch. Cool on cookie sheet 1 minute. Let cool on
wax or parchment paper. Makes 15–20 cookies.

Cooking with My Friends (Kentucky)

Chocolate Marshmallow Cookies

½ cup butter, softened
1 cup sugar
1 egg
1 teaspoon vanilla
¼ cup milk
1¾ cups sifted all-purpose flour
½ teaspoon salt
½ teaspoon baking soda

½ cup cocoa
18–24 marshmallows, cut in half
2 cups sifted powdered sugar
5 tablespoons cocoa
⅛ teaspoon salt
3 tablespoons butter
4–5 tablespoons heavy cream
½ cup pecan halves

Cream butter and sugar. Add egg, vanilla, and milk; beat well. Sift together the flour, salt, baking soda, and cocoa; add to creamed mixture, and blend well. Drop by teaspoon onto cookie sheet. Bake at 350° for 8 minutes; don't overbake. Remove from oven, and press ½ of a marshmallow, cut-side-down, onto each cookie. Bake 2 minutes longer. Cool. Combine powdered sugar, cocoa, salt, butter, and cream; cream together well. Frost tops of cookies, and top with pecan halves. Store in airtight container to keep marshmallows soft.

Sleigh Bells and Sugarplums (Washington)

To easily cut marshmallows, coat a knife, scissors, or pizza wheel with non-stick spray, and gently wipe it. Be sure to wash and re-coat with spray when the cutter gets sticky.

Hawaiian Snowflakes

I serve these all year because they are always a hit and so easy to make. They freeze well, too.

2 egg whites
⅔ cup sugar

1 cup chopped walnuts
1 cup chocolate chips

Preheat oven to 350°. Beat whites until fluffy. Gradually add sugar, and beat until stiff. Carefully fold in nuts and chocolate chips. Drop by teaspoonfuls onto foil-covered cookie sheet. Place in oven, close door, count to ten, and turn oven off. Do not open door until several hours later or the next day when oven has completely cooled. Makes about 4 dozen.

The When You Live in Hawaii You Get Very Creative
During Passover Cookbook (Hawaii)

Fast 'n Fancy Macaroons

1 (14-ounce) can sweetened
condensed milk
2 teaspoons vanilla

1 (14-ounce bag) Baker's Angel
Flake Coconut

Combine ingredients, mixing well. Drop from teaspoon 1 inch apart on well-greased baking sheets. Bake at 350° for 10–12 minutes or until lightly browned. Remove at once from baking sheets, using moistened spatula. Makes about 5 dozen.

Variations: Chocolate-A-Roons: fold in 4 squares semisweet chocolate before baking. Nut-A-Roons: add 1 cup chopped pecans before baking. Raisin-A-Roons: add 1 cup raisins before baking. Chip-A-Roons: add 1 cup chocolate chips before baking.

Calling All Cooks (Alabama)

Chocolate Kiss Macaroons

⅓ cup butter or margarine,
  softened
3 ounces cream cheese, softened
¾ cup sugar
1 egg yolk
2 teaspoons almond extract
2 teaspoons orange juice

1¼ cups all-purpose flour
2 teaspoons baking powder
¼ teaspoon salt
1 (14-ounce) bag flaked coconut
1 (9-ounce) package chocolate
  kiss candies, wrappers removed

One hour before baking, in a large mixing bowl, cream together butter, cream cheese, and sugar until fluffy. Add egg yolk, almond extract, and orange juice, and beat well.

In another bowl, combine flour, baking powder, and salt; gradually add to creamed mixture. Stir in all but ¾ cup coconut. Set remainder aside. Cover, and chill dough 1 hour, or until it can be handled easily.

Preheat oven to 350°. Shape dough into balls 1 inch in diameter, then roll in remaining coconut. Place on an ungreased cookie sheet. Bake 10–12 minutes, or until lightly browned (watch to make sure coconut doesn't burn). Remove from oven; before cookies begin to cool, press an unwrapped chocolate kiss on top of each. Cool 1 minute, then remove to a wire rack to finish cooling. Yields 4–5 dozen cookies.

Red Pepper Fudge and Blue Ribbon Biscuits (North Carolina)

Do you even think of a coconut as being a nut? Indeed, it is the largest of all the nuts, weighing an average of 1½ pounds, and one tree will produce thousands of coconuts over its 70-year life span. Shredded, flaked, or toasted, packaged coconut will keep for six months. The canned variety is usually more moist than the bagged variety. Fresh coconut which lasts about four days after grating (refrigerated), is really moist . . . if you're up to the task.

Chocolate Malt Ball Cookies

¾ cup brown sugar
1 teaspoon vanilla
1⅓ sticks margarine or
   vegetable shortening
1 egg
1¾ cups all-purpose flour

⅓ cup cocoa
½ teaspoon salt (if desired, or
   if shortening is used)
½ cup malted milk powder
¾ teaspoon baking soda
2 cups malted milk balls, crushed

Beat together brown sugar, vanilla, and margarine in large bowl until mixed; beat in egg, and mix well. Mix together flour, cocoa, salt, malted milk powder, and baking soda. Add to creamed mixture, and mix until blended. Stir in malted milk ball pieces. (To crush, put candy in sealed plastic bag, and pound with rolling pin or a heavy spoon.)

Drop onto ungreased cookie sheet by rounded tablespoonfuls 2 inches apart. Best to bake 1 sheet at a time at 375° for 7–9 minutes or until cookies are set. Do not overbake. Cool 2 minutes before removing to sheets of foil to cool completely. Makes about 3 dozen cookies.

In the Kitchen with Kate (Kansas)

Brownies & Squares

Double Dipper Chocolate
Brownies

Double Dipper Chocolate Brownies

2 eggs
1 cup sugar
½ cup butter or margarine,
   melted
1 teaspoon vanilla extract
⅔ cup all-purpose flour

6 tablespoons cocoa
½ teaspoon baking powder
¼ teaspoon salt
1 cup white chocolate chips
1 cup semisweet chocolate chips

Preheat oven to 350°. In large bowl, mix eggs, sugar, melted butter, and vanilla. In separate bowl, combine dry ingredients, and add to egg mixture. Stir gently with spoon to blend. Grease an 8-inch square pan. Stir white chocolate and chocolate chips into batter. Pour into prepared pan. Bake 25–35 minutes. Makes 6–8 servings.

The Table at Grey Gables (Tennessee)

Cream Cheese Fudge Brownies

BATTER:
½ cup shortening
½ cup butter or margarine
4 eggs
2 cups sugar
4 tablespoons cocoa

1 cup all-purpose flour
½ teaspoon salt
1 cup coconut
1 cup pecans
2 teaspoons vanilla

Mix in order given. Spread ⅓ of Batter in greased 9x13-inch pan. Spoon Cream Cheese Filling over it. Spoon remaining Batter over Cream Cheese Filling. Spread carefully. Bake at 350° for 35 minutes.

CREAM CHEESE FILLING:
3 ounces cream cheese, softened
2 tablespoons butter
¼ cup sugar

1 egg
1 tablespoon all-purpose flour
½ teaspoon vanilla

Cream cheese and butter together. Add sugar, a spoonful at a time. Mix well. Add egg, flour, and vanilla. Stir until mixed well.

The Pink Lady . . . in the Kitchen (Arkansas)

Butter Crème Brownies

1 square semisweet chocolate	½ cup sugar
¼ cup butter	¼ cup all-purpose flour
1 egg	¼ cup finely chopped pecans

Melt chocolate and butter together over hot water, and cool slightly. Beat egg until frothy. Stir into chocolate mixture. Add sugar. Blend well. Add flour and nuts, and stir until well blended. Pour into greased 8x8-inch pan. Bake at 350° for 13–15 minutes. Cool, and cover with Butter Crème Filling. Yields 2 dozen.

BUTTER CRÈME FILLING:

1 cup powdered sugar	1 tablespoon heavy cream or
2 tablespoons butter, softened	evaporated milk
¼ teaspoon vanilla extract	

Cream all together, and spread over brownie layer. Put pan in refrigerator for 10 minutes. Remove, and spread with Glaze.

GLAZE:

2 tablespoons butter	2 squares semisweet chocolate

Melt butter and chocolate together. Spread gently over filled brownie layer, being careful not to disturb filling. Chill in refrigerator until Glaze sets. Cut into small finger strips. Can be frozen.

Vintage Vicksburg (Mississippi)

Color adds appeal. Try adding food coloring to Butter Crème Filling for different holidays and occasions.

Best Ever Brownies

2 cups sugar
1 cup vegetable oil
1 teaspoon vanilla
1¾ cups all-purpose flour
½ teaspoon salt
½ cup cocoa
5 eggs
1 cup chopped nuts (optional)
1 cup semisweet chocolate chips

Place all ingredients, except chocolate chips, in large bowl. Mix well with spoon. Pour into greased 9x13-inch baking pan. Sprinkle chips on top, and bake at 350° for 25–30 minutes or until toothpick inserted in center comes out clean. Yields 4–5 dozen squares.

Treat Yourself to the Best Cookbook (West Virginia)

One-Bowl Butterscotch Brownies

These are so easy, they're dangerous. You can add peanut butter chips, chocolate chips, coconut, or anything else you crave.

4 squares unsweetened baker's
   chocolate
¾ cup butter or margarine,
   (not low-fat spreads)
2 cups sugar
3 eggs, beaten
1 teaspoon vanilla
1 cup all-purpose flour
1½ cups coarsely chopped walnuts
   or pecans, divided
2 cups mini marshmallows
1 cup butterscotch morsels

Preheat oven to 350°. Grease a 9x13-inch baking dish, and set aside.

In a large saucepan on low heat, melt together unsweetened chocolate and butter or margarine. Turn off heat, but leave pan on stove while you stir in sugar, then eggs and vanilla. Stir in flour and half the nuts. Spread mixture into pan, and bake 35 minutes. Remove from oven, and resist the temptation to dig in—we're not finished yet!

Immediately sprinkle with remainder of nuts, marshmallows, and butterscotch morsels. Return pan to oven, and bake 3–5 minutes; watch until you see toppings start to melt. Remove from oven, and cool before slicing. Yields 15 large squares or 24 little ones.

Hungry for Home (North Carolina)

Gypsy Raspberry Brownies

¾ cup butter, melted
1½ cups sugar
2 teaspoons vanilla
3 eggs, slightly beaten

¾ cup all-purpose flour
½ cup unsweetened cocoa
½ teaspoon baking powder
½ teaspoon salt

Cream butter, sugar, and vanilla. Beat in eggs. In another bowl, stir together flour, cocoa, baking powder, and salt with fork. Blend dry ingredients into egg mixture. Do not overbeat. Spread batter into ungreased 8-inch square baking pan.

FILLING:
1 (8-ounce) package cream
    cheese, softened
1 egg
½ teaspoon baking powder

1 tablespoon sugar
1 (12-ounce) jar raspberry
    preserves
Powdered sugar

Combine cream cheese, egg, baking powder, and sugar thoroughly. Swirl (use back of spoon to make trenches) cream cheese mixture and raspberry preserves through chocolate batter before baking. Bake 30–40 minutes in preheated 350° oven until brownie pulls away from edges of pan. Cool completely. Dust with powdered sugar, and cut into squares. Makes 9.

Raspberry Enchantment House Tour Cookbook (New Mexico)

Raspberry preserves come in different-sized jars. One popular seedless variety is 10 ounces, and that will do just fine whenever the ounces specified is close.

Fudgy Chocolate Cookie Bars

1¾ cups all-purpose flour
¾ cup powdered sugar
¼ cup Hershey's cocoa
1 cup cold butter
1 (12-ounce) package chocolate
   chips, divided

1 (14-ounce) can sweetened
   condensed milk
1 teaspoon vanilla
1 cup chopped walnuts

Combine flour, sugar, and cocoa; cut in butter until crumbly (can be done in food processor). Press firmly onto bottom of a 9x13-inch baking dish. Bake 15 minutes at 350°.

Over medium heat, melt 1 cup chocolate chips with condensed milk and vanilla. Pour evenly over crust. Top with nuts and remaining 1 cup chips. Press down firmly. Bake 20 minutes or until set. Cool. Chill. Cut into bars. Store covered. Makes 15–18 bars.

Wapiti Meadow Bakes (Idaho)

Amaretto Cheesecake Cookies

1 cup all-purpose flour
⅓ cup packed brown sugar
6 tablespoons butter, softened
1 (8-ounce) package cream
   cheese, softened

¼ cup sugar
1 egg
4 tablespoons amaretto
½ teaspoon vanilla
4 tablespoons chopped almonds

In a large mixing bowl, combine flour and brown sugar. Cut in butter until mixture forms fine crumbs. Reserve 1 cup crumb mixture for topping. Press remainder over bottom of ungreased 8-inch square baking pan. Bake for 12–15 minutes at 350° or until lightly browned.

In mixer bowl, thoroughly cream together cream cheese and sugar. Add egg, amaretto, and vanilla; beat well. Spread batter over partially baked crust. Combine almonds with reserved crumb mixture; sprinkle over batter. Bake for 20–25 minutes. Cool, and cut into squares. Yields 16 bar cookies.

Dining on Deck (Vermont)

Cherry-Filled White Chocolate Squares

½ cup butter
2 cups vanilla chips, divided
2 eggs
½ cup sugar
1 cup all-purpose flour

½ teaspoon salt
½ teaspoon almond extract
½ cup cherry jam or preserves
½ cup shredded coconut
¼ cup sliced almonds

In a small saucepan, melt butter over low heat. Remove from heat, and add 1 cup vanilla chips; do not stir.

In a mixing bowl, beat eggs, and gradually add sugar until blended; stir in vanilla chip mixture. Add flour, salt, and extract, and stir well. Spread ½ of batter in a greased and floured 8x8-inch baking pan. Bake at 325° for 20 minutes.

In a small saucepan, melt jam over low heat, then spread evenly over baked mixture. Top with remaining batter, remaining vanilla chips, coconut, and almonds. Bake at 325° for 20–25 minutes or until light brown. Allow to cool before cutting into squares. Makes 9 squares.

Ohio Cook Book (Ohio)

Almond extract is such a delightful flavor enhancer—especially to chocolate and cherry. Try subbing it or adding it to the more popularly used vanilla when you feel adventurous.

Moca Java Bars

A yummy blend of flavors.

BOTTOM LAYER:

1¼ cups all-purpose flour
1 teaspoon sugar
1 teaspoon baking powder
Dash of salt
1¼ sticks butter

2 tablespoons strong coffee, cold
1 egg yolk
1 (12-ounce) package chocolate
  chips

Preheat oven to 350°. Lightly grease a 10x15-inch jellyroll pan. Combine flour, sugar, baking powder, and salt in a large bowl. Cut in butter until mixture resembles coarse crumbs. In a small bowl, mix coffee and egg yolk, blending well. Stir into flour mixture and moisten to form dough. Press onto bottom of pan. Bake 10 minutes. Remove, and sprinkle chocolate chips over top; return to oven for 2 minutes. Remove, and evenly spread chocolate with a spatula. Allow to stand several minutes.

TOP LAYER:

1 stick butter, softened
1 cup sugar
1 tablespoon vanilla
2 eggs plus 1 egg white

2 tablespoons strong coffee
1 cup chopped nuts
Powdered sugar for dusting

Cream butter, sugar, and vanilla. Beat in eggs and egg white, one at a time. Add coffee (mixture will appear slightly curdled). Stir in nuts, and spread over Bottom Layer. Return to oven, and bake 20–25 minutes, or until top is brown. Remove, and dust with powdered sugar. Cool in pan, and cut into bars. Yields 3 dozen bars.

Three Rivers Renaissance Cookbook IV (Pennsylvania)

Toffee Butter Bars

These are extremely easy to make, yet earn rave reviews everywhere!

1 cup butter, softened
1 cup sugar
1 egg
1 teaspoon vanilla extract
2 cups self-rising flour

1½–2 (7-ounce) bars Hershey
   Special Dark Chocolate, broken
   into squares
½ cup (or more) finely chopped
   walnuts or pecans

Preheat oven to 350°. Grease a 9x13-inch baking pan. Cream butter and sugar until fluffy. Beat in egg and vanilla. Gradually add flour, mixing well. Spread mixture in prepared pan. Bake for 20 minutes (cookie bottom may not appear done, but is fully baked). Place chocolate squares on top of cookie bottom immediately after removing from oven. When chocolate is melted, spread evenly with spatula. Sprinkle on nuts. Immediately cut into bars. Makes 24 bars.

California Sizzles (California)

Brickle Bars

½ cup butter or margarine
2 squares (2 ounces)
   unsweetened chocolate
1 cup sugar
2 eggs

1 teaspoon vanilla
¾ cup all-purpose flour
¾ cup almond brickle pieces
½ cup miniature semisweet
   chocolate pieces

In a 2-quart saucepan, cook and stir butter or margarine and unsweetened chocolate over low heat until melted. Remove from heat; stir in sugar. Add eggs and vanilla; beat lightly with a wooden spoon just until combined (don't overbeat, as brownies will rise too high, then fall). Stir in flour.

Spread batter in a greased 8x8x2-inch baking pan. Sprinkle almond brickle pieces and chocolate pieces evenly over batter. Bake in 350° oven for 30 minutes. Remove pan from oven, and cool brownies in pan on a wire rack. Cut into bars. Makes 16 bars.

Home Cookin' is a Family Affair (Connecticut)

Marshmallow Krispie Bars

1 (14-ounce) package caramels
¾ cup margarine, divided
1 (14-ounce) can sweetened
   condensed milk

2 (10-ounce) packages miniature
   marshmallows, divided
8 cups crisp rice cereal

Melt unwrapped caramels with ¼ cup margarine and condensed milk in saucepan over low heat, stirring to mix well; set aside. Melt remaining ½ cup margarine and 1½ packages marshmallows in saucepan over low heat, stirring to mix well. Pour over cereal in large bowl; mix well. Press half the mixture in buttered 10x15-inch dish. Sprinkle with remaining ½ package marshmallows. Spread caramel mixture over marshmallows. Top with remaining half cereal mixture. Let stand until firm. Cut into bars. Yields 70 servings.

Y Cook? (North Dakota)

Peanut Squares

You can count on kids loving these . . . and adults' fingers reaching for them as well.

CRUST:

1½ cups all-purpose flour
⅔ packed brown sugar
½ teaspoon baking powder
½ teaspoon salt
¼ teaspoon baking soda

½ cup butter, softened
1 teaspoon vanilla
2 egg yolks
3 cups miniature marshmallows

Heat oven to 350°. Combine all Crust ingredients except marshmallows. Press firmly in bottom of ungreased 9x13-inch pan. Bake at 350° for 12–15 minutes or until light golden brown; remove from oven. Immediately sprinkle with marshmallows. Return to oven for 1–2 minutes or until marshmallows just begin to puff. Cool while preparing Topping.

TOPPING:

⅔ cup corn syrup
½ cup butter
2 teaspoons vanilla
1 (12-ounce) package peanut
   butter chips

2 cups crisp rice cereal
2 cups salted peanuts

In large saucepan, heat corn syrup, butter, vanilla, and peanut butter chips until chips are melted and mixture is smooth; stir constantly. Remove from heat; stir in cereal and peanuts. Immediately spoon warm Topping over marshmallows; spread to cover. Refrigerate until firm. Cut into bars.

Centennial Cookbook (Wisconsin)

Peanut Butter Bites

½ cup creamy or crunchy
    peanut butter
¼ cup unsalted butter,
    softened
1¼ cups sugar
2 large eggs, lightly beaten

1 teaspoon vanilla extract
2 cups all-purpose flour
1 teaspoon baking powder
½ teaspoon salt
1 cup chopped peanuts, plus
    more for garnish

Heat oven to 350°. Line a 9x13-inch baking pan with foil; generously coat with nonstick cooking spray.

In medium-size bowl, beat together peanut butter and butter. Beat in sugar until well blended; beat in eggs and vanilla. Stir in flour, baking powder, and salt. Add peanuts (mixture will be stiff). Press batter evenly into prepared pan. Bake in 350° oven 30 minutes or until bar pulls away from sides of pan. Let cool completely in pan on wire rack.

PEANUT BUTTER FROSTING:
½ cup creamy peanut butter
¼ cup unsalted butter, softened
½ cup powdered sugar

In medium-size bowl, beat together peanut butter, butter, and powdered sugar until smooth and fluffy. Spread over top of cooled bar. Sprinkle with chopped peanuts, if desired, and cut into 36 rectangles.

Cooking with Love & Memories (North Carolina)

It's a safer choice to buy creamy peanut butter to have on hand for recipes (or children). If you want crunchy, simply take out a little of the peanut butter, and add some chopped peanuts.

Lemon Crumb Squares

1 (14-ounce) can sweetened
   condensed milk
1 teaspoon grated lemon rind
½ cup lemon juice
1½ cups all-purpose flour

½ teaspoon salt
1 teaspoon baking powder
1 cup uncooked oatmeal
⅔ cup butter, softened
1 cup dark brown sugar

Blend milk, lemon rind, and juice for filling. Set aside. Sift together flour, salt, and baking powder; stir in oatmeal. Cream butter and sugar. Mix with flour mixture until crumbly. Spread half the mixture in buttered pan; pat down. Spread condensed milk mixture over it. Cover with remaining crumbly mixture. Bake at 350° for about 25 minutes. Cool in pan for 15 minutes. Cut into squares. Chill in pan until firm.

Recipes for Lori's Lighthouse (Florida)

Pecan Pie Bars

2 cups all-purpose flour
½ cup powdered sugar
1 cup butter or margarine
1 (14-ounce) can sweetened
   condensed milk

1 egg
1 teaspoon vanilla extract
Pinch of salt
1 cup toffee-flavored chips
1 cup chopped pecans

In mixing bowl, combine flour and sugar. Cut in butter until mixture resembles coarse meal. Press firmly into a greased 9x13-inch pan at least 2 inches deep. Bake at 350° for 15 minutes. Meanwhile, in another bowl, beat milk, egg, vanilla, and salt. Stir in toffee chips and pecans. Spread evenly over baked crust. Bake for another 20–25 minutes or until lightly browned. Cool, then refrigerate. When thoroughly chilled, cut into bars. Store in refrigerator. Makes 4 dozen.

The Pure Food Club of Jackson Hole (Wyoming)

Coconut Lime Bars

1 cup butter or margarine,
   softened
¼ teaspoon salt
½ cup powdered sugar
2¼ cups all-purpose flour,
   divided

4 eggs, slightly beaten
1 tablespoon grated lime peel
5 tablespoons fresh lime juice
2 cups sugar
1 cup flaked coconut

Preheat oven to 350°. Combine butter, salt, powdered sugar, and 2 cups flour in a bowl, mixing to make a soft dough. Press evenly into an ungreased 9x13-inch baking pan. Bake for 15–20 minutes or until golden.

Combine eggs, lime peel, lime juice, sugar, and remaining ¼ cup flour in a bowl; blend until smooth. Spoon over crust. Sprinkle coconut over lime mixture. Reduce oven temperature to 325°. Bake for 25 minutes or until firm. Cool. Cut into bars. Yields 3 dozen bars.

Dining by Design (California)

Lime Pecan Bars

These bars are a very popular treat at Moosewood. They have a chewy cookie crust topped with a sweet lime custard. Only freshly squeezed lime juice will provide zing without bitterness. If you can't resist the flavor of limes, you will definitely want to use the optional lime peel, although these bars are excellent without it.

CRUST:

½ cup pecans

¼ cup butter, melted

¾ cup unbleached white flour

⅓ cup packed brown sugar

Preheat oven to 325°. Butter a nonreactive 8-inch square baking pan. In the bowl of a food processor or by hand, finely chop pecans. Add melted butter, flour, and brown sugar, and process or blend with your fingers to form a crumbly mixture. Press the crust into prepared pan, and bake 25–30 minutes until golden brown.

TOPPING:

3 large eggs

1 cup sugar

½ cup fresh lime juice

⅓ cup unbleached white flour

2 teaspoons finely grated lime peel (optional)

12 pecan halves, toasted (optional)

Whisk together the eggs and sugar. Stir in lime juice, flour, and lime peel, if using, and mix well until smooth. When crust is baked, pour the lime custard into it, and return the pan to the oven. Bake for about 20 minutes, until the topping is firm to the touch. Cool in the pan for about 1 hour. Cut into 12 pieces, and gently press a pecan half into the center of each piece, if desired. Remove the bars with a spatula to a serving plate or storage container. Yields 12.

Note: Wash and finely grate the peels of 3 or 4 limes before juicing them. If the limes are hard, soften them before peeling by rolling them on a counter with the heel of your hand, tossing them in a game of catch with your children, or throwing them on the floor. No kidding! They'll yield more juice.

Moosewood Restaurant Book of Desserts (New York)

Lime Pecan Bars

Pineapple Squares

Have a taste of Hawaii in this moist, delicious pineapple treat.

½ cup (1 stick) butter or
   margarine, softened
1⅓ cups sugar
4 eggs
1½ cups all-purpose flour
1 teaspoon baking powder

½ teaspoon baking soda
¼ teaspoon salt
1 (20-ounce) can crushed
   pineapple, drained
Powdered sugar for garnish

Cream together butter and sugar with an electric mixer for 2 minutes on HIGH speed. Mix in eggs. Add dry ingredients, except the powdered sugar, and mix.

Drain pineapple (can reserve juice for another use). Add pineapple to the batter, and stir with a spoon until blended. Pour into a greased, 9x13-inch pan, and bake for 30–35 minutes at 350°. Cool; cut into 24 bars. Sprinkle with powdered sugar.

Aunty Pua's Keiki Cookbook (Hawaii)

Don't throw that good pineapple juice away. It is great to add to orange or other juices. Also, it acts like lemon juice to keep apple and banana slices from browning in other recipes.

Buttery Apple Squares

Great lunch box or picnic treats.

2 cups plus 2 tablespoons
   all-purpose flour, divided
1 teaspoon salt
⅔ cup plus 1 tablespoon butter,
   chilled, divided
1 egg yolk

½ cup milk
5 medium Rome Beauty apples,
   peeled, thinly sliced (5 cups)
¾ cup sugar
1 teaspoon cinnamon
1 egg white, slightly beaten

Preheat oven to 375°. Sift 2 cups flour and salt into bowl. Cut in ⅔ cup butter till mixture resembles large peas. Add a mixture of the egg yolk and milk, mixing just till moistened. Divide dough into 2 equal portions, and pat one of the portions over the bottom of a greased 7x10-inch baking pan. Spread apples in prepared pan.

Mix remaining 2 tablespoons flour, sugar, and cinnamon in a small bowl. Sprinkle over apples and dot with remaining 1 tablespoon butter. Roll remaining dough on a lightly floured surface. Place it over the apples; seal edges, and cut vents. Brush lightly with egg white. Bake at 375° for 1 hour or till crust is light brown and apples are tender.

VANILLA FROSTING:

½ cup powdered sugar
2 tablespoons light cream or milk

½ teaspoon vanilla extract

Combine all ingredients in bowl, and mix well. Spread over warm apple dessert. Cut into squares to serve. Serves 10–12.

The Dexter Cider Mill Apple Cookbook (Michigan)

Creamy Almond Puff Bars

Creamy Almond Puff Bars

This is so delicious you'll have to hide it till you are ready to serve it!

2 sticks (1 cup) butter, divided
2 cups all-purpose flour, stirred
　and measured, divided
1 cup plus 2 tablespoons water,
　divided

1 teaspoon almond extract
3 large eggs
Sliced almonds for garnish

Cut 1 stick butter into 1 cup flour, as for pastry. Add 2 tablespoons water; mix with fork until ball forms. Divide. On large ungreased jellyroll pan, pat each portion into a 3x12-inch strip, spacing strips about 3 inches apart.

In a saucepan, bring 1 cup water and other stick of butter to a boil. When butter is melted, stir in remaining 1 cup flour all at once, and stir vigorously until mixture pulls away from sides of pan to gather into a smooth ball. Remove from heat. Add almond extract. Add eggs, one at a time, beating each into the dough until well incorporated and smooth. Divide dough in half and spread each half onto one pastry strip. Bake at 350° for one hour or until golden brown. Cool. Spread with Almond Cream Cheese Frosting, and garnish with sliced almonds. Slice diagonally. Serves 8–10.

ALMOND CREAM CHEESE FROSTING:
4 ounces cream cheese, softened
½ cup butter, softened

2½ cups powdered sugar
½ teaspoon almond extract

In large bowl, cream the cheese and butter until smooth. Gradually beat in the sugar and almond extract. Beat until of spreading consistency, adding a little evaporated milk, if necessary.

Only the Best (Utah)

Coconut Chews

¾ cup shortening (or half butter
   or margarine, softened)
¾ cup powdered sugar
1½ cups plus 2 tablespoons
   all-purpose flour, divided
2 eggs

½ teaspoon baking powder
½ teaspoon salt
½ teaspoon vanilla
½ cup chopped walnuts
½ cup flaked coconut

Heat oven to 350°. Cream shortening and powdered sugar. Blend in 1½ cups flour. Press evenly in bottom of ungreased 9x13x2-inch baking pan. Bake 12–15 minutes.

Mix remaining ingredients, including remaining 2 tablespoons flour; spread over hot baked layer, and bake 20 minutes longer. While warm, spread with Orange-Lemon Icing. Cool. Cut into bars. Makes 32 cookies.

ORANGE-LEMON ICING:

1½ cups powdered sugar
2 tablespoons butter or
   margarine, melted

3 tablespoons orange juice
3 teaspoons lemon juice

Mix until smooth and of spreading consistency.

Cookie Exchange (Colorado)

Nuts are often interchangeable—especially walnuts and pecans—and can generally be used according to taste, and what you have on hand.

Frosted Raisin Bars

2 cups seedless raisins
1 teaspoon baking soda
1½ cups sugar
3½ cups all-purpose flour
1 cup butter, softened

2 teaspoons cinnamon
⅛ teaspoon salt
1 teaspoon vanilla
2 eggs

Cover raisins with water in saucepan; bring to a boil. Let cool 20 minutes. Add enough water to raisin juice to equal 1 cup. Add baking soda. Add remaining ingredients all at once; stir till well blended. Spread very thin on 2 large, greased and floured cookie sheets. Bake at 350° for 15–18 minutes. Frost while hot. Makes 60–70 bars.

BUTTER FROSTING:
2 cups powdered sugar
¼ cup butter, melted

½ teaspoon salt

Mix all ingredients well with enough water for spreading consistency. Spread over raisin bars while they are hot.

Heirloom Recipes and By Gone Days (Ohio)

Lulu's Lip Smackin' Shortbread

2 cups all-purpose flour
½ cup powdered sugar
¼ teaspoon salt
¼ teaspoon baking powder

1 teaspoon vanilla extract
1 cup butter or margarine,
  softened
2 tablespoons sugar

Preheat oven to 350°. In a mixer bowl, combine flour, powdered sugar, salt, baking powder, vanilla, and butter; beat at medium speed until well mixed. Pat dough into 9-inch round pan, and prick well with fork. Sprinkle sugar over dough. Bake 30–35 minutes. Cut into wedges while warm, and cool on wire rack. Separate the cookies. Makes 6–10 cookies.

Kitchen Komforts (Tennessee)

Fruit and Cheese Pizza

Everybody loves this. It's as simple as that. And gorgeous.

1 (20-ounce) package refrigerated
   sugar cookie dough
1½ (8-ounce) packages
   cream cheese, softened
⅓ cup plus 2 tablespoons sugar
3 tablespoons brandy or
   orange juice, divided

1 teaspoon vanilla extract
4 cups (more or less) thinly sliced
   fruit
¼ cup berries
½ cup fruit preserves (any flavor)

Preheat oven to 375°. Lightly spray a 14-inch pizza pan with vegetable spray. Cut cookie dough into ¼-inch thick rounds. Arrange in slightly overlapping pattern on prepared pan, covering pan completely. (Flour your hands before you start working with the dough to make this all go much easier.) Press dough together to seal. Make a ridge on edges of crust with your fingers (to hold the filling). Bake until puffed and golden, about 10 minutes. Cool completely.

Combine cream cheese, sugar, 1 tablespoon brandy, and vanilla in bowl. Spread evenly over crust. Arrange fruit in circular pattern over filling. Put berries in center. Melt preserves with remaining 2 tablespoons brandy in small saucepan over low heat. Brush over fruit. Chill for at least an hour before serving. Serves 8–10.

Angel Food (North Carolina)

Fruit and Cheese Pizza

Chocolate Cookie Pizza

½ cup plus 2 tablespoons
   butter, softened, divided
½ cup brown sugar
¼ cup sugar
1 teaspoon vanilla
1 egg
1¼ cups all-purpose flour
½ teaspoon baking soda

3 tablespoons milk
1 cup chocolate chips
1 cup powdered sugar
½ cup pecan halves
½ cup M&M's
¼ cup shredded coconut
2 ounces white chocolate,
   melted

Preheat oven to 350°. In a large bowl, combine ½ cup butter, brown sugar, sugar, vanilla, and egg until well combined. Add flour and baking soda to make a stiff dough. Pat dough onto an ungreased 12-inch pizza pan or baking sheet. Bake in oven 15 minutes or until golden brown. Remove cookie from oven, and let cool.

In a saucepan over very low heat, combine remaining 2 tablespoons butter, milk, and chocolate chips. Heat, stirring frequently, until chocolate is melted. Remove chocolate mixture from heat, and stir in powdered sugar. Beat until smooth. If frosting is not glossy, stir in a few drops of hot water. Spread frosting over baked and cooled cookie. Immediately decorate with pecan halves, M&M's, and coconut. Press toppings lightly into frosting. Drizzle melted white chocolate over toppings. Let stand until set. If desired, remove from pan and cut into wedges. Makes 12–16 slices.

Down Home Cooking Done Right (North Carolina)

Chocolate chips are hard to find in 6-ounce packages anymore, so we are specifying "1 cup" instead. If you buy a 12-ounce package, you will have 2 cups. I usually estimate half the bag, as these little chippies don't have to be measured perfectly . . . and anyway, some have been known to disappear!

Mose's Buttermilk Pie

People sometimes turn up their noses at the sound of buttermilk pie, so don't tell them what it is . . . just wait for their waves of compliments. You'll wish you'd made two.

3 eggs
1 cup sugar
2 tablespoons flour
1 stick butter, melted

1 teaspoon vanilla
1 cup buttermilk
1 (9-inch) pie shell

Beat eggs. Add dry ingredients, and mix well. Add butter, vanilla, and buttermilk. Pour into pie shell and bake at 350° for 30–45 minutes or until custard is set. Custard will continue to firm after baking.

Top O' the Morning (Alabama)

Granny's Buttermilk Coconut Pie

1¼ cups sugar
3 eggs
¾ stick margarine, melted
½ cup buttermilk

1 teaspoon vanilla
1 cup flaked coconut
1 (9-inch) unbaked pie shell

Mix together sugar, eggs, margarine, buttermilk, vanilla, and coconut, and pour in unbaked pie shell. Bake at 350° for 25–30 minutes or until it shakes done.

Editor's Extra: In any custard pie such as this, prevent a soggy crust by brushing the uncooked shell with a slightly beaten egg white, then bake at 425° for about 10 minutes. Fill, and bake according to recipe.

Feeding His Flock (Mississippi)

Pecan Pie

A classic.

1 cup light corn syrup
1 cup light brown sugar
3 eggs
2 teaspoons vanilla

¼ teaspoon salt
1 stick butter
1 cup chopped pecans
1 (9-inch) pie crust

Mix all but the pecans together until smooth, then add pecans. Pour into an unbaked pie shell. Cook at 350° for 50–60 minutes. Serves 6–8.

La Bonne Louisiane (Louisiana)

Brushing pie crust with milk or egg wash before baking adds a nice rich color to a pie. To give it even more shine, thin two tablespoons light corn syrup with hot water. After the pie is baked, brush the thinned syrup over the crust. You can further give it sparkle by sprinkling some sugar—colored, if you like—over the top. Put pie back in oven for two minutes to let glaze dry and set.

Bourbon Pecan Butterscotch Pie

A different version of the southern favorite pecan pie.

1 (9-inch) unbaked pie shell	**1 cup sugar**
⅔ cup butterscotch chips	**⅛ teaspoon salt**
3 eggs	**1 teaspoon vanilla**
½ cup sour cream	**2 ounces bourbon**
½ cup dark corn syrup	**1¾ cups chopped pecans**

Preheat oven to 400°. Cover bottom of pie shell with butterscotch chips. In a medium-size mixing bowl, combine eggs, sour cream, corn syrup, sugar, salt, vanilla and bourbon. Mix well to blend ingredients, until mixture is smooth. Add pecans. Pour into the pie shell with chips. Place in oven, and immediately turn down temperature to 350°. Bake for 50 minutes or until firm, and a knife comes out clean when inserted in the center. Serves 8.

Note: If using extra large or jumbo eggs, use a 10-inch pie plate. If a less sweet pie is desired, sugar may be reduced to ¾ cup.

Virginia Wine Country (Virginia)

Upside-Down Apple Pecan Pie

Even if this doesn't turn out perfectly from the pan, it tastes so good, you don't care how uniform your slice is.

4 tablespoons butter
⅔ cup brown sugar
⅔ cup pecan halves
2 (9-inch) unbaked pastry
  circles

1 tablespoon all-purpose flour
½ teaspoon nutmeg
½ teaspoon cinnamon
6 cups peeled and sliced apples
1 tablespoon lemon juice

Combine butter and brown sugar. Spread mixture evenly on the bottom of a 9-inch pie plate (be sure to butter rim of pie plate). Arrange pecan halves in design, pressing into sugar. Cover with plain pastry. Trim, leaving ½ inch hanging over all around.

Combine flour, nutmeg, and cinnamon with apples and lemon juice; pile onto pastry, leveling as much as possible. Cover with second crust. Fold edges from first pastry and prick with a fork on top. Bake at 450° for 10 minutes. Reduce to 350°, and bake for 30–45 minutes or longer, until done to your liking. When syrup in pan stops bubbling (about 5 minutes), place serving plate over pie and invert. Remove pie plate. Serve with vanilla ice cream. Serves 16.

A Gracious Plenty (West Virginia)

Red Inn Apple Pie

This unusual recipe appears to have no crust. However, the custard forms a kind of crust under the apples. It is delicious and so easy to make!

7 Granny Smith apples, pared   **Pinch of cinnamon**
  and thinly sliced   **Pinch of nutmeg**

Butter a 10-inch pie plate. Sprinkle the sliced apples with cinnamon and nutmeg, and mix together. Place the apples in the pie plate.

CUSTARD:
2 eggs   **½ cup Bisquick**
1 cup sugar   **¾ cup milk**

Beat together the ingredients for the Custard, and pour it over the apples.

CRUMBLE:
1 cup Bisquick   **3 tablespoons butter (hard)**
⅓ cup brown sugar   **Heavy cream**
½ cup chopped walnuts

Mix together the ingredients for the Crumble, and cut in the butter. Sprinkle this over the apples, and press down lightly. Bake in a preheated oven at 325° for 1 hour. Serve with whipped cream. Serves 6–8.

A recipe from The Red Inn, Provincetown
A Taste of Provincetown (Massachusetts)

Refrigerate pies containing eggs (pumpkin, custard, cream pies); however, they don't freeze well. Fruit pies can be kept at room temperature or stored in frig, loosely covered, for two days. You can freeze a baked fruit pie up to four months. Freeze uncovered till frozen, then wrap tightly and return to freezer. To serve a double-crusted fruit pie, unwrap and thaw at room temperature one hour; heat pie at 375° on the lowest oven rack 35–40 minutes.

Apple Pie with Sour Cream

2 tablespoons plus ⅓ cup
   all-purpose flour, divided
¾ cup plus ⅓ cup sugar, divided
1¼ teaspoons cinnamon,
   divided
⅛ teaspoon salt
1 egg

½ teaspoon vanilla
1 cup sour cream
6 medium-size apples,
   peeled, cored and sliced
1 (9-inch) pie shell, unbaked
   and chilled
¼ cup butter

Preheat oven to 400°. In a bowl, sift together 2 tablespoons flour, ¾ cup sugar, ¾ teaspoon cinnamon, and salt. Stir in egg, vanilla, and sour cream. Fold in the apples, and spoon mixture into pie shell. Bake 15 minutes, then reduce oven temperature to 350°, and bake 30 minutes longer.

Meanwhile, combine the remaining flour, sugar, and cinnamon. With a pastry blender or fingertips, blend in the butter until mixture is crumbly. Increase the oven temperature to 400°. Sprinkle crumb mixture over the pie, and bake 10 minutes longer. Serves 8.

German Recipes (Iowa)

Fried Apple Pies

This recipe comes from the Pioneer Crafts Festival held in Rison annually. It has been a festival secret for over 70 years!

8 ounces dried apples slices	**1 teaspoon cinnamon**
5 cups water	**2½ tablespoons cornstarch**
1 cup sugar	**2 tablespoons lemon juice**

Cook apples in water for 20 minutes. Combine sugar, cinnamon, and cornstarch. Add to apples. Add lemon juice. Cook until thickened. Cool.

PASTRY:

1 cup plus 2 tablespoons shortening	**7 tablespoons water**
3 cups all-purpose flour	**1 teaspoon salt**
1 egg, beaten slightly	**1 teaspoon vinegar**

Cut shortening into flour. Combine egg, water, salt, and vinegar. Pour into flour mixture, and mix.

Pinch small amount of dough, and roll out on floured board.

Cut out circles, using a 5-inch saucer as a guide. Put 1 tablespoon apple mixture on dough. Wet edges of dough with iced water. Fold dough over apple mixture, and seal by pressing a floured fork around edges. Fry in 1–2 inches of oil in a skillet on medium-high setting. Cook until golden brown, turning only once. Glaze with a mixture of powdered sugar and water. Yields about 12–16 pies.

A Great Taste of Arkansas (Arkansas)

Fried Apple Pies

Peaches and Cream Streusel Pie

STREUSEL:

⅓ cup firmly packed dark
   brown sugar
⅓ cup all-purpose flour
⅓ cup old-fashioned rolled oats
½ teaspoon ground cinnamon

¼ teaspoon ground nutmeg
¼ cup chilled butter, cut into
   small pieces
¼ cup sliced almonds (about 1
   ounce)

Preheat oven to 350°. In a medium bowl, mix together brown sugar, flour, oats, cinnamon, and nutmeg. Using a pastry blender or 2 butter knives, cut the butter into the flour mixture until coarse crumbs form. Stir in almonds.

FILLING:

1 large egg
⅓ cup heavy cream
¼ cup sugar
1 teaspoon vanilla

1 teaspoon almond extract
½ teaspoon ground nutmeg
Pinch of salt

Mix egg, cream, sugar, vanilla, almond extract, nutmeg, and salt.

5 cups ripe, peeled, pitted, and
   sliced peaches (about 1½
   pounds)

1 (8-inch) pie shell, baked

Arrange the sliced peaches in the bottom of baked pie shell; pour Filling over peaches. Sprinkle Streusel evenly over the cream mixture to edges of pie crust. Press Streusel down slightly. Bake pie until the Streusel is lightly browned, 30–35 minutes. Transfer pan to a wire rack to cool completely. Garnish with peach slices.

Note: If using frozen peaches, you will need 1 pound of unsweetened frozen, thawed, drained peaches.

Recipes to Make You Purr (Wyoming)

Peacheesy Pie

PEACHES 'N' CHEESECAKE FILLING:

1 (29-ounce) can peach slices
½ cup sugar
2 tablespoons cornstarch

2 tablespoons corn syrup
2 teaspoons pumpkin pie spice
2 teaspoons vanilla

Drain peaches; save syrup. Mix peaches, sugar, cornstarch, corn syrup, pumpkin pie spice, and vanilla.

CHEESECAKE TOPPING:

2 eggs, slightly beaten
⅓ cup sugar
1 tablespoon lemon juice

3 ounces cream cheese, softened
½ cup yogurt or sour cream

Combine eggs, sugar, lemon juice, and 2 tablespoons peach syrup in small saucepan. Cook, stirring constantly until thick. Blend cream cheese with yogurt. Add hot mixture, and beat till smooth.

CRUST:

⅔ cup shortening
2 cups all-purpose flour, sifted
1 teaspoon salt

6–7 tablespoons peach syrup
2 tablespoons margarine

Cut shortening into mixture of flour and salt until size of peas. Sprinkle peach syrup over mixture, stirring until dough holds together. Roll out, and fit into 9-inch pie pan. Fill with peach mixture. Dot with butter. Cover with Cheesecake Topping. Roll out remaining dough. Cut into circles. Brush with peach syrup, and arrange on Cheesecake Topping. Bake at 425° for 10 minutes, then cover edge with foil. Bake at 350° for 30–35 minutes. Serves 8–10.

The Parkview Way to Vegetarian Cooking (Maine)

Easy Pear Pie

This recipe is a little different from most pie recipes, but it is my favorite kind of recipe —easy and delicious!

3 or 4 fresh, ripe pears	2 eggs
1 (9-inch) unbaked pie crust	1 teaspoon lemon juice
1 cup sugar	½ teaspoon vanilla
1 cup all-purpose flour	½ teaspoon ground ginger
¼ cup butter, melted	

Preheat oven to 400°. Wash and drain pears. Cut pears (peeled or un-peeled) lengthwise into halves; remove core, and stem ends with paring knife. Arrange pears cut-side-down in pie shell, with wide ends of pears near outside edge of shell; set aside. Beat sugar, flour, butter, eggs, lemon juice, vanilla, and ginger with electric mixer till smooth and blended. Pour into pear-lined shell.

Bake for 40–45 minutes, or till golden brown and top springs back when lightly pressed with finger. Serve warm. Refrigerate any left-overs. Serves 6.

Good Food from Michigan (Michigan)

Rhubarb Cheesecake Pie

3 cups chopped rhubarb, cut into ½-inch pieces	1 tablespoon all-purpose flour
½ cup sugar	1 (9-inch) unbaked pie shell

Toss rhubarb with ½ cup sugar and flour. Add to pie shell. Bake in preheated 425° oven for 15–20 minutes.

CHEESE TOPPING:

2 eggs	1 (8-ounce) package cream cheese, softened
1 cup sugar	

Beat eggs with sugar and cream cheese until smooth. Pour over rhubarb. Reduce heat to 350° and continue baking for 30 minutes. Cool before serving. Makes 6–8 servings.

Merrymeeting Merry Eating (Maine)

Great Fresh Strawberry Pie

I pull this recipe out every June during strawberry season. It is the best fresh strawberry pie I've ever had.

CRUST:

1½ cups all-purpose flour
2 tablespoons sugar
2 tablespoons cold milk
½ teaspoon salt

½ cup Mazola corn oil
  (for some reason no other
  kind of oil will work)

Blend ingredients together, and pat by hand into 9-inch pie pan. Bake in a 450° oven for about 10 minutes; the Crust will be starting to brown. Cool Crust, then fill.

(This Crust is super easy and very flaky. The taste is slightly sweet. It can be used for other 1-crust pie recipes, and is especially good when the filling is slightly tart.)

FILLING:

1 quart fresh, ripe strawberries
1 cup sugar
2 well-rounded tablespoons
  cornstarch

2 tablespoons white Karo syrup
1 cup water
2 tablespoons strawberry Jell-O

Clean, and drain strawberries. In a saucepan, blend together sugar and cornstarch. Slowly mix in syrup and water, stirring well so there are no lumps. Cook until the mixture is thick and clear.

Remove from heat, and add 2 tablespoons strawberry Jell-O dry mix. Stir until Jell-O is dissolved. Immediately add strawberries to hot Filling, and stir in. When Filling has begun to cool, pour into Crust. Refrigerate. Serves 8.

Editor's Extra: Real whipped cream is our favorite to top slices, but any kind will do.

Aspic and Old Lace (Indiana)

Lime Pie in Meringue Crust

Lime Pie in Meringue Crust

A light, airy, and tart dessert. The meringue crust and lime custard are a heavenly combination. Allow for seconds, or at least be prepared to allow your guests to lick the pie plate.

5 eggs, at room temperature, separated
¼ teaspoon cream of tartar
¾ cup sugar
⅛ teaspoon salt
⅓ cup sugar
⅓ cup freshly squeezed lime juice
2 tablespoons grated lime peel
2 cups whipping cream, divided
Lime slices for garnish

Preheat oven to 275°. Grease a 10-inch pie plate, and set aside. In a large bowl, beat egg whites with cream of tartar until soft peaks form. Slowly add ¾ cup sugar, a little at a time, beating until stiff and glossy. Spoon meringue into prepared pie plate, mounding it up side and over edge. Bake 1 hour, and cool at room temperature.

To prepare filling, beat egg yolks and salt in a medium-size bowl until fluffy. Whisk in ⅓ cup sugar, lime juice, and peel, and place mixture in top of a double boiler over boiling water. Whisk constantly until thick and smooth, about 10 minutes. Remove from heat, and let cool.

Beat 1 cup whipping cream until stiff. Fold this into cooled lime custard, and pour into cooled meringue shell. Refrigerate pie at least 4 hours.

Serve garnished with additional cup of whipping cream, whipped, and lime slices. Serves 8.

Tony Clark's New Blueberry Hill Cookbook (Maine)

Ann's Lemon Pie

FILLING:

1¼ cups sugar
6 tablespoons cornstarch
2 cups water
3 egg yolks (reserve whites
   for Meringue)

⅓ cup lemon juice
½ teaspoon lemon extract
2 teaspoons vinegar
3 tablespoons butter
1 (9-inch) pie shell, baked

Mix sugar and cornstarch; add water. Combine egg yolks with lemon juice; beat. Add to sugar mixture. Cook in double boiler for 25 minutes, until thick. Add lemon extract, vinegar, and butter. Pour into pie shell.

MERINGUE:

1 tablespoon cornstarch
2 tablespoons cold water
½ cup hot water
3 egg whites

3 tablespoons sugar
1 teaspoon vanilla
⅛ teaspoon salt

Mix cornstarch with cold water. Add hot water, and boil until thick. Cool. Beat egg whites until foamy. Stir in sugar, vanilla, and salt. Add cornstarch mixture, and beat on high speed until stiff peaks form. Spread over Filling, and bake at 350° for 10 minutes.

Our Best Home Cooking (Washington)

For pretty slices, coat knife with butter before cutting a meringue pie. But even when a grandchild "slices" this pie . . . well, you get the picture.

Ann's Lemon Pie

Sweet Potato Custard Pie

1 cup mashed cooked sweet
   potatoes
1 cup sugar
2½ tablespoons butter, melted
2 eggs, separated

1 teaspoon vanilla
1½ cups scalded milk
Pinch of nutmeg
1 (9-inch) deep-dish pie shell,
   or 2 (9-inch) pie shells

Mix potatoes, sugar, and butter; beat well. Add egg yolks, vanilla, milk, and nutmeg; beat together well. Beat egg whites stiff, adding them last; stir well. Pour into pie shell(s). Bake at 400° for 30 minutes, then reduce heat to 350° for 20 minutes (deep dish may take longer). Test for doneness with a knife. Serves 8.

Come, Dine With Us! (Maryland)

Pumpkin Pie

By the legendary Grand Ole Opry star, Minnie Pearl, this is an old favorite.

¾ cup brown sugar
1 tablespoon all-purpose flour
½ teaspoon salt
2¼ teaspoons pumpkin pie spice

1½ cups canned pumpkin
1⅓ cups evaporated milk
1 egg, slightly beaten
1 (8-inch) unbaked pastry shell

Preheat oven to 375°. Combine brown sugar, flour, salt, and spice. Stir in pumpkin, milk, and egg; mix till smooth. Pour into unbaked pastry shell.

Bake about 25 minutes. Remove from oven, and spread Nut Topping around edge. Bake 15 minutes more. Serve warm or cold.

NUT TOPPING:
½ cup chopped pecans
1½ teaspoons orange zest

1 tablespoon butter
2 tablespoons brown sugar

Combine all ingredients. Use as directed. Makes 6 servings.

Minnie Pearl Cooks (Tennessee)

Quick Eggnog Pie

1 envelope unflavored gelatin
3 tablespoons cold water
2 cups commercially prepared
  eggnog
1 cup heavy cream, whipped
¼ cup sugar

¼ teaspoon salt
2 teaspoons vanilla or rum
  flavoring
1 (9-inch) graham cracker
  pie shell
Nutmeg for garnish

Soften gelatin in cold water. Warm eggnog over direct low heat. Stir in softened gelatin, and continue heating until completely dissolved. Chill until partially set, then beat until smooth.

Into stiffly whipped cream, beat sugar, salt, and flavoring. Fold into eggnog mixture. Pour into pie shell. Chill 2–4 hours. Garnish with nutmeg. Serves 8.

A Hancock Community Collection (New Hampshire)

Peanut Butter Pie

The meringue is the perfect top-off to a great pie.

1 cup powdered sugar
½ cup chunky peanut butter

1 (9-inch) pastry shell, baked

Blend sugar and peanut butter with fork until mixture is crumbly. Spread ½ mixture in bottom of baked pastry shell; reserve remainder.

FILLING:
¼ cup cornstarch
⅔ cup sugar
3 eggs, separated
½ teaspoon vanilla

1 tablespoon peanut butter
¼ teaspoon salt
2 cups milk

Combine cornstarch, sugar, egg yolks (reserve whites), vanilla, peanut butter, salt, and milk, and cook in double boiler until thickened, stirring constantly. Spoon Filling over peanut butter mixture in pastry shell.

MERINGUE:
3 reserved egg whites
3 tablespoons sugar

½ teaspoon salt

Beat egg whites, sugar, and salt until stiff and spread over pie. Sprinkle remaining peanut butter mixture on top. Bake at 325° for 20 minutes, or until Meringue is firm and brown. Serves 8.

More . . . Home Town Recipes (West Virginia)

Godiva Chocolate Pie

Our customers' all-time favorite dessert!

½ cup butter
3 ounces Godiva chocolate,
   or 3 ounces milk chocolate
4 eggs
3 tablespoons white corn syrup
1½ cups sugar
¼ teaspoon salt

¼ cup milk
1 teaspoon vanilla extract
1 (9-inch) pie shell, unbaked
Ice cream (optional)
Whipping cream, whipped
   (optional)

Preheat oven to 350°. Melt butter and chocolate in top of double boiler. Set aside to cool. Beat eggs until light and thick. Add next 5 ingredients. Add chocolate and butter mixture. Mix well. Pour into pie shell. Bake 30–35 minutes or until top is crusty and filling is set. Do not overbake. This pie does not need meringue. Pie can be served warm and topped with ice cream or whipped cream. Serves 8–10.

Fessin' Up with Bon Appétit (Louisiana)

Candy Bar Pie

5 (2-ounce) Snickers candy bars
1 (9-inch) pie shell, baked
½ cup sugar
12 ounces cream cheese, softened
2 eggs

⅓ cup sour cream
⅓ cup peanut butter (crunchy
   or smooth)
⅔ cup semisweet chocolate chips
2 tablespoons whipping cream

Cut candy bars into ¼-inch pieces. Place candy bar pieces in baked pie shell; set aside. In a mixing bowl, beat sugar and cream cheese until smooth. Add eggs, sour cream, and peanut butter; beat on low speed just until combined. Pour mixture into pie shell; smooth over candy pieces. Bake at 350° for 35–40 minutes or until set. Cool on wire rack.

In small heavy saucepan, melt chocolate chips in whipping cream until smooth, spread over cooled pie filling, and refrigerate overnight. Serves 8.

Jefferies Relay Team: Generating a Cure (South Carolina)

Little Chess Tarts

An elegant bite of something sweet.

CREAM CHEESE PASTRY:

1 (8-ounce) package cream
   cheese, softened
2 sticks butter, softened

2 cups all-purpose flour

Mix cream cheese and butter; add flour ½ cup at a time, blending thoroughly. Use your fingers to mix it well. Refrigerate for ½ hour or more.

FILLING:

1 stick butter, softened
1½ cups sugar
2 eggs
2 tablespoons cornmeal
2 tablespoons all-purpose flour

1 cup light cream
2 tablespoons lemon juice
½ teaspoon vanilla
Pinch of salt
Damson (plum) preserves

Cream butter and sugar; beat in eggs. Mix cornmeal with flour and add other ingredients except preserves. Beat well.

Pinch off small pieces of pastry and form into balls about 1¼ inches in diameter. Put in 1½-inch greased muffin pans and press dough evenly to line the bottom and sides. Fill half full, and bake at 350° for 14–20 minutes till filling is brown around the edge. Remove from pans and place on rack to cool. Top each tart with a tiny bit of damson preserves. These freeze well. Makes 48.

The Farmington Cookbook (Kentucky)

Though the origin is debatable, one commonly stated theory is that damsons were first cultivated in antiquity in the area around the ancient city of Damascus, capital of modern-day Syria, and were introduced into England by the Romans. If you can't find something that says "damson," any plum preserves—or any other flavor, for that matter—will work just fine.

Little Chess Tarts

Mocha Macaroon Pie

The four C's guarantee this a winner: chocolate, coffee, coconut, and cream. Yum.

5 egg whites
1 cup minus 2 tablespoons
   sugar
1 teaspoon vanilla
2 teaspoons instant coffee
½ teaspoon almond extract

6 ounces grated unsweetened
   chocolate
1 cup graham cracker crumbs
¼ cup flaked coconut
1 teaspoon baking powder

Whip egg whites at high speed until it forms soft peaks. Add sugar, vanilla, coffee, and almond extract, and whip to stiff peaks. Fold in gently by hand the chocolate, cracker crumbs, coconut, and baking powder. Pour into a greased and floured 9-inch springform pan, and bake at 350° for 30–35 minutes. Allow to cool.

FILLING:

1½ cups heavy cream
¼ cup powdered sugar
1 tablespoon instant coffee

1 teaspoon vanilla
½ teaspoon almond extract

After pie is completely cool, combine Filling ingredients, and whip until stiff. Spread over pie.

TOPPING:

2 tablespoons grated chocolate

2 tablespoons toasted coconut

Sprinkle grated chocolate and coconut over Filling. Serves 8–10.

Peter Christian's Recipes (Maine)

Desserts

My Favorite Peach Cobbler

My Favorite Peach Cobbler

This makes a big cobbler . . . and it doesn't last long.

CRUST:

2 cups all-purpose flour
1–1½ cups sugar
4 teaspoons baking powder
½ teaspoon salt
1½ cups milk
1 teaspoon vanilla

Combine flour, sugar, baking powder, and salt. Stir in milk and vanilla; set aside.

FILLING:

2 quarts peach slices, drained
½ stick butter
2 teaspoons lemon juice
½ cup sugar
3 tablespoons cornstarch
  or clear gel
¾ cup water

In saucepan, bring first 4 Filling ingredients to a boil. Mix together cornstarch and water to make a paste; gradually add to Filling mixture. Pour into 3-quart Pam-sprayed baking dish, then pour Crust mixture evenly over top.

TOPPING:

1 stick butter
¼ cup sugar
1 teaspoon cinnamon

Melt butter, and pour over Crust. Mix together sugar and cinnamon; sprinkle over top. Bake at 350° for 40 minutes. Serve warm with milk. Serves 10.

Montezuma Amish Mennonite Cookbook I (Georgia)

White Peach and Raspberry Cobbler

Toward the end of July or the beginning of August, there is nothing better than finding perfectly ripe, fragrant white peaches at a farmstand in Ulster or Dutchess County. At that time in summer, raspberries are sure to be close by. Pick up a good supply of both so you have some left to make this cobbler when you get home.

3 very ripe peaches, peeled and   **1 cup raspberries**
    sliced (yellow will do)   **3 tablespoons sugar**

In a 1½- to 2-inch shallow, flameproof casserole, combine the peaches and raspberries with sugar. Preheat oven to 350°.

BATTER:
½ cup sugar   **1 tablespoon unsalted butter,**
1¼ cups all-purpose flour   **melted**
2 teaspoons baking powder   **½ cup milk**

In a bowl, combine sugar, flour, and baking powder; mix in butter and milk. Put casserole over medium-low heat and gently heat the fruit, stirring it gently as the sugar melts and the peaches and raspberries begin to give up their juice. When fruit has softened, drop batter by tablespoonfuls into the casserole. Place in oven, and bake for about 35 minutes, until fruit is bubbling and top is firm and lightly browned. Serve on its own, or with whipped cream or vanilla ice cream. Serves 6–8.

The Hudson River Valley Cookbook (New York)

Cherry Cobbler

2 (16-ounce) cans pitted sour
  cherries (see note)
1 cup sugar, divided
2 tablespoons cornstarch
1¼ teaspoons almond extract
1 cup quick or old-fashioned
  oats, uncooked
1 cup all-purpose flour

2 teaspoons baking powder
¼ teaspoon salt (optional)
⅓ cup butter or margarine,
  chilled
½ cup milk
Whipped cream or ice cream
  (optional)

Drain cherries, reserving 1 cup liquid. In medium saucepan, combine ¾ cup sugar and cornstarch; stir in reserved liquid. Bring to a boil over medium heat. Stir constantly until thickened and clear. Reduce heat. Boil 1 minute. Stir in cherries and extract. Pour mixture into a greased 8-inch square glass baking dish. Heat oven to 400°. Combine oats, flour, remaining ¼ cup sugar, baking powder, and salt; mix well. Cut in butter until mixture resembles coarse crumbs. Add milk, and mix with fork just until dry ingredients are moistened. Drop by rounded tablespoons over hot filling. Bake 25–30 minutes or until topping is light golden brown. Serve warm with whipped cream or ice cream, if desired. Serves 8–10.

Note: May substitute 2 (20-ounce) cans cherry pie filling and omit ¾ cup sugar and 2 tablespoons cornstarch.

Christ Reformed Church Historical Cookbook (West Virginia)

Unlike a pie, a cobbler never contains a bottom crust, but has biscuits or pie crust on top. Cobblers originated in Colonial America by English settlers unable to make their suet puddings for lack of ingredients and cooking equipment, so instead covered a stewed filling with biscuits or dumplings fitted together. The cooked surface has the appearance of a cobbled street.

Buttermilk-Crusted Blackberry Cobbler

FILLING:

1½ **pounds blackberries**
1⅓ **cups sugar**

3½ **tablespoons all-purpose flour**
1⅓ **tablespoons vanilla extract**

In a medium bowl, combine blackberries, sugar, flour, and vanilla. Pour into greased 8x12x2-inch pan.

CRUST:

1 **tablespoon plus 2½ teaspoons**
   sugar
¾ **teaspoon baking powder**
¼ **teaspoon salt**

⅓ **cup shortening**
½ **cup buttermilk**
1⅓ **cups all-purpose flour, divided**
½ **tablespoon melted butter**

Preheat oven to 350°.

In a large bowl, stir together 1 tablespoon sugar, baking powder, salt, shortening, buttermilk, and ¾ cup flour to form a sticky dough. Spread remaining flour on a work surface, and knead dough until most of the flour is incorporated and dough is manageable. Roll dough to about ¼-inch thickness, and cut with a knife into large pieces. Cover blackberry filling with dough, overlapping pieces. Drizzle melted butter over dough, and sprinkle with remaining 2½ teaspoons sugar.

Bake until crust is golden brown and filling is bubbly, about 50 minutes. Serves 8–10.

By Request (Arizona)

Blueberry Buckle
with Cinnamon Bourbon Sauce

FIRST LAYER:

1 cup butter, room temperature
⅓ cup sugar
1 egg, beaten
2 cups all-purpose flour

2 teaspoons baking soda
1 cup buttermilk
2 pints blueberries

Preheat oven to 350°. Grease and flour 9x11-inch pan. Cream butter and sugar until light and fluffy; beat in egg. Sift flour with baking soda. Stir dry ingredients, alternating with buttermilk into cream mixture. Spread mixture in prepared dish. Cover with berries.

SECOND LAYER:

1 cup all-purpose flour
½ cup sugar
½ cup packed brown sugar
½ cup toasted pecans

½ cup unsalted butter, cut in
    pieces
½ teaspoon nutmeg
¼ teaspoon ginger

Combine all ingredients until crumbly. Crumble over berries. Bake 1 hour until brown.

CINNAMON BOURBON SAUCE:

½ cup butter
¾ cup sugar
2 eggs
½ teaspoon cinnamon

1 tablespoon very hot water
½ cup whipping cream
½ cup bourbon

Melt butter over simmering heat in a double boiler. Beat sugar, eggs, and cinnamon in bowl, then add to butter; add water, stirring until mixture coats back of spoon (7 minutes). Remove from heat; cool to room temperature. Beat in whipping cream and bourbon. Serve squares of Blueberry Buckle topped with warm Cinnamon Bourbon Sauce. Serves 10–12.

Blueberry Pride: Blueberry Bash Recipes 1989–1993 (Alaska)

Trifle Bowl

Trifle Bowl

This is incredibly beautiful, and always a hit. You can't go wrong.

1 angel food cake, crumbled in
    chunks
2–3 bananas, sliced
1 (20-ounce) can chunk
    pineapple, drained
1 (6-ounce) package vanilla
    instant pudding mix

1 (10-ounce) package frozen
    strawberries (or fresh)
1 (12-ounce) carton Cool Whip
Blueberries (optional)

Layer ½ of angel food cake in bottom of trifle bowl. Next, layer ½ of sliced bananas and pineapple chunks. Prepare pudding according to directions on package, and layer ½ on top. Repeat layers of above ingredients. Top with strawberries, Cool Whip, and blueberries, if desired. Serves 12.

Note: Blueberries and strawberries may be added in layers, if desired.

Family Treasures (South Carolina)

Easy Chocolate Mint Mousse

1 (6-ounce) package chocolate-
    covered mints
1 cup semisweet chocolate chips
⅓ cup sugar

3 eggs
1 cup milk
1 cup whipping cream

Place mints, chocolate chips, sugar, and eggs in blender. Scald milk. Add hot milk slowly to blender. Blend until smooth. Pour into bowl. Chill until it begins to set.

Whip cream, and fold into chocolate mixture. Spoon into sherbet dishes and chill until set. This is very rich. Yields 8–10 servings.

Prescriptions for Good Eating (South Carolina)

Rhubarb Crunch

CRUMB CRUST/TOPPING:

1 cup sifted all-purpose flour
¾ cup uncooked rolled oats
1 cup brown sugar

½ cup butter, melted
1 teaspoon cinnamon

Combine ingredients until crumbly. Press half of crumbs into greased 9-inch pan, reserving half for top.

FRUIT MIXTURE:

4 cups sliced rhubarb
1 cup sugar
2 tablespoons cornstarch

1 cup water
1 teaspoon vanilla

Place sliced rhubarb in crust. In a small saucepan, combine sugar, cornstarch, water, and vanilla. Cook, stirring until thick and clear. Pour over rhubarb. Cover with reserved crumbs. Bake at 350° for 1 hour.

The Ruby Valley Friendship Club Cookbook II (Nevada)

Walnut Apple Crisp

5 cups tart apples, sliced
2 tablespoons lemon juice
¼ cup water
½ cup all-purpose flour
½ cup rolled oats

1 cup packed brown sugar
1 teaspoon nutmeg
Dash of salt
½ cup butter, softened
1 cup coarsely chopped walnuts

Toss apples with lemon juice and water in a shallow 2-quart baking dish. In large bowl, combine flour, oats, sugar, nutmeg, and salt. Mix to blend thoroughly. With a pastry blender, cut in butter until mixture resembles coarse crumbs. Mix in walnuts. Crumble over apples to cover completely. Do not pack down.

Bake in 350° oven for 40–45 minutes or until top is lightly browned. Serve warm or at room temperature. Accompany with ice cream, or pour cream over, if you wish. If top turns dark too fast, cover baking pan loosely with foil. Serves 6–8.

Cook Book (California)

Praline Crème Brûlée

2 cups heavy cream	1 teaspoon vanilla
3 large egg yolks	¼ cup firmly packed brown sugar
¼ cup sugar	¼ cup finely chopped pecans

Preheat oven to 300°. Scald cream (heat to just before a boil). Beat egg yolks with sugar and vanilla until sugar has dissolved. Stir in hot cream. Strain into 6 ramekins. Place ramekins in a roasting pan, and pour hot water halfway up sides of ramekins. Bake in water bath for 20–25 minutes or until just set. Remove from water bath, and cool.

Heat broiler. Mix together brown sugar and pecans, and sprinkle in an even layer over top of custards. Place under broiler 5–6 inches from heat until topping has melted and caramelized. If sugar begins to burn, move ramekins further away from heat. The caramelizing will take 4–5 minutes. Allow to cool, then chill well before serving.

Recipes and Remembrances (Florida)

Wow! Ice Cream

1½ teaspoons pure almond extract	1½–2 cups fresh black cherries, pits and stems removed, coarsely chopped
1 cup toasted slivered almonds	
8 ounces mini-chocolate chips	1 batch your favorite vanilla ice cream recipe

Add first 4 ingredients to vanilla ice cream base. Churn as usual. For an added treat, top scoops of ice cream with Ganache.

GANACHE:

12 ounces chocolate chips	1 cup heavy cream

Microwave 1½ minutes; stir, and continue microwaving until smooth.

Aliant Cooks for Education (Alabama)

Editor's Extra: You can use softened bought ice cream, then refreeze after mixing.

Cherry Chewbilees

1¼ cups all-purpose flour
½ cup brown sugar
½ cup shortening
½ cup flaked coconut
1 cup chopped walnuts, divided
2 eggs

2 (8-ounce) packages cream
   cheese, softened
⅔ cup sugar
2 teaspoons vanilla
2 (21-ounce) cans cherry pie
   filling

Preheat oven to 350°. Combine flour and brown sugar. Cut in short-ening with pastry blender till fine crumbs form. Add coconut and ½ cup nuts. Set aside ½ cup of crust mixture. Press remaining crust mixture in greased 9x13-inch pan. Bake 12–15 minutes till edges are slightly browned.

Beat eggs, cream cheese, sugar, and vanilla till smooth. Spread over crust. Bake 15 minutes more. Spread cherry pie filling on top.

Combine remaining ½ cup nuts with reserved crust mixture; sprin-kle over cherries. Bake 15 minutes to toast nuts. Cool. Refrigerate several hours. Pretty to scoop into a bowl. Serves 12–15.

Recipes & Remembrances (Utah)

Strawberry Lasagna

2 (8-ounce) packages cream
  cheese, softened
2 (3-ounce) boxes vanilla
  instant pudding mix
½ cup powdered sugar
1 cup milk

8 cups mashed strawberries
¼ cup Kirsch (cherry brandy)
1 cup sugar
2 loaves pound cake
1 cup whipping cream, whipped

Beat cream cheese, pudding mix, powdered sugar, and milk in a mixer bowl at high speed until smooth. Combine strawberries, Kirsch, and sugar in medium bowl, mixing well. Remove 1 cup strawberry mixture. Purée in a food processor, and reserve for garnish.

Slice pound cakes into ½-inch slices. Line a 9x13-inch dish with ⅓ of the cake slices. Layer ⅓ cream cheese mixture, ⅓ strawberry mixture, and half remaining cake in prepared dish. Layer half remaining cream cheese mixture, half remaining strawberry mixture, remaining cake, and remaining cream cheese mixture in prepared dish. Swirl remaining strawberry mixture over top. Chill 4–8 hours.

Cut dessert into 3-inch squares to serve. Top with reserved strawberry purée and whipped cream. Serves 10.

Taste of the Town (Tennessee)

A Little Touch of Heaven

⅔ cup chopped almonds
6 tablespoons butter, melted
2 cups crushed vanilla wafers
2 teaspoons almond extract

3 pints vanilla ice cream,
  softened, divided
1 (10- to 20-ounce) jar apricot
  preserves, divided

Combine almonds, butter, wafers, and almond extract. Cover bottom of 8-inch square pan with half the crumb mixture. Cover with ½ of ice cream, and ½ of preserves. Add half of remaining crumbs, remaining ice cream, and remaining preserves. Top with remaining crumbs. Freeze. Remove from freezer 15 minutes before serving. Cut into squares. Makes 10–12 servings.

Second Round: Tea-Time at the Masters® (Georgia)

Layered Blueberry Dessert

COOKIE LAYER:

1 cup margarine, softened   1 cup chopped walnuts
1 cup all-purpose flour

Cut margarine into flour until crumbly. Add chopped nuts. Pat into a 9x13-inch pan. Bake at 350° for 10–12 minutes. Cool.

CREAM LAYER:

1 (8-ounce) package cream   1 cup powdered sugar
   cheese, softened   1 (8-ounce) container Cool Whip

Whip cream cheese with powdered sugar. Fold in Cool Whip. Place on cooled cookie layer in dabs; spread carefully to level. Chill well.

BERRY LAYER:

1 cup sugar   3 tablespoons dry raspberry Jell-O
4 tablespoons cornstarch   1 quart fresh or frozen blueberries
1 cup water (or berry juice with   1 (8-ounce) container Cool Whip
   enough water to measure 1 cup)

Blend sugar with cornstarch in saucepan. Add water. Boil over medium heat until thick and clear, stirring constantly. Add Jell-O, and stir until completely dissolved. Add fresh or frozen blueberries; remove from heat. Partially chill berry mixture to prevent melting cheese layer. Spread Berry Layer over Cream Layer. Chill well. Spread Cool Whip over top to serve.

Nome Centennial Cookbook 1898–1998 (Alaska)

Layered Blueberry Dessert

Old-Fashioned Strawberry Shortcake at its Best

Serve in large individual bowls, and enjoy!

1½–2 quarts fresh strawberries, divided
½ cup sugar

2 tablespoons Grand Marnier (or orange juice)
½ teaspoon vanilla

Rinse strawberries; let dry. Hull, and set aside 6 large ones. In food processor or blender, purée half of remaining berries with sugar, Grand Marnier, and vanilla. Slice remaining berries, and stir into purée. Cover, and let stand 20 minutes, or make ahead and refrigerate for no more than 6 hours. If refrigerated, let warm to room temperature before serving.

SHORTCAKE:

2¼ cups all-purpose flour
6 tablespoons sugar
1½ teaspoons baking powder
¾ teaspoon baking soda
⅛ teaspoon salt
1½ teaspoons orange zest

½ cup chilled butter or margarine, cut in pieces
¾ cup buttermilk
Extra sugar for sprinkling on top
1 cup heavy (whipping) cream

Preheat oven to 400°. Combine flour, sugar, baking powder, baking soda, salt, and orange zest in large bowl. Cut in chilled butter with pastry blender (or forks) until mixture resembles coarse crumbs. Add buttermilk, tossing with fork, until mixture can be gathered into a ball.

Roll dough out on a floured surface to about 1-inch thickness. The dough may then be cut into 6 rounds with large cookie cutter, or cut into squares. Sprinkle with sugar, place on lightly greased cookie sheet, and bake for 20–25 minutes or until done. (These may be made ahead and reheated for a few minutes in a 250° oven.) Cool shortcakes slightly; split them.

Whip cream. Spoon strawberries over bottoms, replace tops, and spoon more berries over. Serve with whipped cream and reserved whole berries. This dessert is best served in large individual bowls. Serves 6.

Wandering & Feasting (Washington)

Charlotte au Chocolat

This is our house dessert that we have been serving since we opened, using candied violets as a garnish. It continues to rank among our most popular desserts.

1 (8-ounce) package semisweet
   chocolate
1 cup sugar
½ cup brewed coffee, hot

½ pound butter, softened
4 eggs, beaten
2 tablespoons liqueur of your
   choice, if desired

Grate chocolate. Add sugar and hot coffee. Add butter and eggs, and mix together well. Mix in liqueur, if desired.

    Line an 8–10 cup charlotte mold or soufflé pan with double-folded, heavy-duty aluminum foil. Pour in batter. Bake at 350° for 45 minutes to 1 hour. Chill. Serve covered with piped whipped cream or crème chantilly. Serves 8.

Note: We did this in a smaller soufflé dish for 35 minutes without tin foil. Also beautiful in a fence of lady fingers in a springform pan.

A recipe from Upstairs At The Pudding, Cambridge
A Taste of Boston (Massachusetts)

Warm Chocolate
Brownie Cups

Warm Chocolate Brownie Cups

These individual cakes with an oozing, velvety chocolate center will delight the child in everyone. They can be made ahead of time and refrigerated until the next day, or frozen.

6 ounces bittersweet chocolate, chopped
¾ cup unsalted butter
3 eggs, at room temperature
3 egg yolks, at room temperature
6 tablespoons sugar
1 tablespoon pure vanilla extract

½ teaspoon salt
5 tablespoons all-purpose flour
¼ cup ground pecans (optional)
Crème fraîche, fresh raspberries, and fresh mint sprigs for garnish

Preheat oven to 375°. Butter and flour 6 (6-ounce) custard cups or ramekins. Set aside. In a medium saucepan, melt chocolate with butter over low heat. Let cool slightly. In a medium bowl, combine eggs, egg yolks, and sugar. Beat until mixture is pale and a slowly dissolving ribbon forms on the surface when beaters are lifted, about 10 minutes. Mix in vanilla and salt. Beat in flour and pecans, if desired. Add chocolate mixture, and beat until thick and glossy, about 5 minutes. Pour batter equally into the cups or ramekins. (At this point, the cups or ramekins can be covered with plastic wrap and refrigerated or frozen until future use.)

Remove cups or ramekins from refrigerator or freezer, and place immediately in preheated oven. Bake until each cake is set around the edges, but moves slightly in center, about 10 minutes, or 15 minutes if frozen; do not overbake. Let cool slightly. Run a knife around edges, and invert onto dessert plates. Garnish each with a dollop of crème fraîche, fresh raspberries, and a mint sprig. Serves 6.

San Francisco Flavors (California)

Warm Chocolate Bliss

⅔ cup bittersweet chocolate
   chips
¼ cup Kentucky bourbon
⅔ cup sugar

½ cup unsalted butter, melted
3 eggs, well beaten, room
   temperature

Preheat oven to 350°. Generously butter a small 6-inch soufflé dish or 2 ramekins; set aside. Put the tea kettle or a pan of water on to warm. Put chocolate chips in a mixing bowl. Mix bourbon and sugar together in a small, heavy-bottomed saucepan. Bring to a boil over medium heat; stir to dissolve sugar. Remove from heat, and pour over chocolate chips (if you use mini-chips, they will melt faster). Stir until chocolate is melted and mixture is completely blended.

Add melted butter; blend in. Add eggs, and whisk briskly to incorporate fully. Pour into buttered small soufflé dish or 2 ramekins. Cover with foil, and put in larger, oven-proof pan. Pour hot water into pan, filling about ¾ of the way up the dish or ramekins. Bake 30 minutes for the single dish, 20–25 for 2 smaller dishes.

Remove from water bath, remove foil, and allow to cool 5 minutes. Invert onto serving plate, and top with ice cream; dust with cinnamon or cocoa powder to serve. Yields 2–4 servings.

Racing to the Table (Kentucky)

Tiger Butter

1 pound white almond bark coating

1 cup peanut butter
2⅓ cups semisweet chocolate chips

Over hot water, or in the microwave, melt together almond bark and peanut butter. While melting, butter a jellyroll pan (or if you want thicker pieces of candy, use a 9x13-inch pan). Stir peanut butter mixture until well blended. Pour into prepared pan. Melt chocolate chips in the same container used to melt first mixture. Pour over the peanut butter layer. Swirl mixture together with a knife. Chill well. Cut into small squares.

Note: This candy may be made in any amount. I usually make about ¼ recipe, pour it into a small pan, and cut it into chunks.

Something Special Cookbook (Oklahoma)

Chocolate Turtles

1 cup semisweet chocolate chips
1 (3½-ounce) jar marshmallow crème
1 cup pecan halves

2¼ cups sugar
½ (12-ounce) can evaporated milk
¼ cup butter or margarine

Combine chocolate chips, marshmallow crème, and pecans in bowl, stirring gently by hand. Combine sugar, evaporated milk, and butter in a saucepan. Cook, stirring constantly, over low heat, until mixture comes to a boil. Cook 7½ minutes. Remove from heat, pour over chocolate mixture, and mix well. Drop by heaping teaspoonfuls onto wax paper. Let stand until firm. Makes 55.

Call to Post (Kentucky)

Chocolate Yule Log

On the screened porch, which is the best refrigerator at Christmas, is our Christmas dessert, the Chocolate Yule Log. I first saw this as an illustration in the "Gourmet Cookbook," a Mother's Day present long ago. It was beautiful . . . a light chocolate roll filled with whipped cream and iced with mocha icing. The garnishes of icing from the pastry tube, the little chocolate twigs, the nuts on top make this so spectacular looking that we use it all year round . . . a Lincoln log in February and chocolate log when we have twelve for dinner and need one dessert that will feed that many.

I have changed the recipe so that it scarcely resembles the original, but it is quickly made and a great favorite. For grown-ups, we sometimes flavor the icing with rum or brandy but our children don't like it, so at Christmas we just use the chocolate and coffee flavors. Don't let the long recipe scare you. One night Susan and I had to make six and had a fresh one in the oven every twenty minutes.

6 eggs, separated	**¼ cup cocoa**
¼ teaspoon cream of tartar	**¼ cup all-purpose flour**
1 cup sugar, divided	**½ teaspoon salt**
1 teaspoon vanilla	

Beat egg whites with cream of tartar till stiff. Gradually add ½ cup sugar, and beat till stiff and glossy. In another bowl, beat egg yolks, and gradually add remaining ½ cup sugar; add vanilla. Sift dry ingredients, and quickly fold into yolk mixture. Fold in egg whites.

Fit a piece of foil into a 10x15-inch cookie sheet. Grease foil with oil. Pour in batter, and smooth out. Bake at 325° for 20–25 minutes. When done, turn out on cup towel (like linen), peel off foil, and roll up from short side while warm, just as you would jellyroll. Let cool all rolled up.

WHIPPED CREAM FILLING:

2 cups whipping cream	**1 teaspoon sugar (or more)**

First chill the beaters and small bowl of mixer in the freezer. This makes the cream whip faster and to a smoother texture. Whip cream, and sweeten with sugar. Set aside in refrigerator till time to fill the roll.

(continued)

(Chocolate Yule Log continued)

MOCHA ICING:

1 teaspoon instant coffee	Pinch of salt
3 tablespoons water (or rum or brandy)	1 tablespoon cocoa
	¼ cup butter, softened
3 cups powdered sugar	⅓ cup chopped pecans (optional)

Dissolve instant coffee in water. Sift sugar, salt, and cocoa together. Blend both mixtures together with butter in mixer till fluffy. You may have to add more sugar to get the right consistency.

Unroll the chocolate roll, fill with Whipped Cream Filling, and roll up again. Carefully place on platter. Ice with Mocha Icing. If you want to, cut off one slice of the roll and break into three pieces. Roll up each of these to make mock twigs to garnish the iced roll. It is pretty, but not necessary to put some of the icing in a paper cone and run through a large star pastry tube to decorate the edges of the roll. Sprinkle chopped pecans on top, if desired. Serves 12.

Chattanooga Cook Book (Tennessee)

Jambalaya Bread Pudding

Jambalaya Bread Pudding

Feeds a crowd. The sauce pours on the magic.

1 (1½-foot) loaf French bread	2 tablespoons vanilla
1 quart milk	1 teaspoon cinnamon
3 eggs, beaten	1 cup raisins
2 cups sugar	3 tablespoons butter

Preheat oven to 375°. In a large bowl, break bread into bite-size pieces. Cover with milk, and soak 1 hour. Mix well. Add eggs and sugar. Stir in vanilla, cinnamon, and raisins. Melt butter in a 9x13x2 baking dish, tilting to coat all sides. Pour in pudding, and bake 45 minutes or till done. Serves 12.

BOURBON SAUCE:

1 stick butter	1 egg, beaten
1 cup sugar	¼ cup bourbon

In top of a double boiler, melt butter and sugar. Gradually whisk in egg. Cool slightly. Add bourbon. If serving right away, pour warm Sauce over pudding. If not, warm Sauce slightly before serving, and serve in a sauce boat.

Jambalaya (Louisiana)

This recipe is easy to halve and bake in an 8x8-inch baking dish for about 35 minutes. In Louisiana, the sauce makes it a celebration.

Milk Chocolate Banana Crème Brûlée

2 cups milk
2 cups heavy cream
¼ cup sugar
5 ounces milk chocolate,
    chopped

½ cup rum
¼ teaspoon mace
¼ teaspoon cinnamon
10 egg yolks, beaten
3 bananas

Combine milk, cream, and sugar, and bring to a boil. Add chocolate, and whisk until blended. Reduce rum by half in separate pan. Add spices to rum, and blend into cream mixture; whisk until blended. Temper in egg yolks.* Slice bananas, and place in bottom of ramekins. Pour custard into ramekins; bake in water bath at 275° about 25 minutes or until set in center.

After custard is complete, chill approximately 3 hours. Sprinkle top of custards with sugar, and burn with a torch (or put under broiler for approximately 15 seconds). Serve immediately. This custard is best served the day it is made. Serves 4–6.

*To temper eggs: Beat eggs, then mix them with a small amount of hot mixture that has been slightly cooled, mixing quickly until completely blended. Then blend this entire mixture back into the larger mixture. This prevents the eggs from curdling, resulting in a smoother sauce.

Recipe from Bound'ry, Nashville
Fine Dining Tennessee Style (Tennessee)

If you choose, sprinkle bananas lightly with lemon or pineapple juice to deter browning. It may alter the taste slightly—we think for the better.

Breakfast Sweets

Cappuccino-Chocolate Coffeecake

Cappuccino-Chocolate Coffeecake

⅓ cup flaked coconut
¼ cup chopped nuts
½ cup sugar, divided
3 tablespoons butter or
    margarine, melted, divided
2 cups Bisquick mix

⅔ cup milk
1 egg
⅓ cup semisweet chocolate chips,
    melted
2 teaspoons powdered instant
    coffee

Heat oven to 400°. Grease an 8x8-inch square pan. Mix coconut, nuts, ¼ cup sugar, and 1 tablespoon butter. Set aside. Beat remaining ingredients (including remaining sugar and butter), except chocolate chips and coffee, in large bowl on low speed 30 seconds, scraping bowl constantly. Beat on medium speed 4 minutes, scraping bowl occasionally. Pour into pan.

Stir together chocolate and coffee; spoon over batter. Lightly swirl chocolate mixture through batter several times with knife for marbled effect. Sprinkle coconut mixture evenly over top. Bake 20–25 minutes or until golden brown. Serve warm. Serves 6–8.

Food for Thought (Ohio)

Some recipes, especially older ones, tell you to melt chocolate over hot water, and that works fine. But microwaving it is so much easier—one to two minutes! Small amounts melt quicker, so just start with a minute, then stir. If you feel any lumps, put it back for another twenty seconds or so, and stir till smooth.

Mendocino Streusel Coffeecake

If you're looking for a light coffeecake with, as professional bakers would say, just the right "crumb," this is it. From Margaret Fox of Mendocino's Café Beaujolais, named more than once the best place to eat breakfast in California.

STREUSEL:

¾ cup packed brown sugar

1 tablespoon ground cinnamon

2 tablespoons fine instant coffee
  powder

3 tablespoons cocoa powder

1 cup finely chopped walnuts

Stir brown sugar with cinnamon, coffee powder, cocoa, and walnuts; set aside.

COFFEECAKE:

2¾ cups all-purpose flour

1½ teaspoons baking powder

1½ teaspoons baking soda

½ teaspoon salt

12 tablespoons (1½ sticks) butter,
  room temperature

2 teaspoons vanilla extract

1½ cups sugar

3 eggs

1 pint sour cream

Powdered sugar for garnish

Heat oven to 375°. Butter and flour a 10-inch Bundt pan, or coat it with a nonstick cooking spray. Stir flour with baking powder, baking soda, and salt; set aside. Beat butter with an electric mixer until light and fluffy. Add vanilla and sugar; beat mixture 3 minutes. Add eggs, and beat at high speed 5 minutes, until mixture is light and creamy. Alternately add flour mixture in 3 additions, using lowest speed of mixer, and sour cream in 2 additions, beating only until smooth after each addition.

Spread a thin layer of batter in bottom of prepared pan. Sprinkle with ⅓ of Streusel mixture. Continue making these layers until there are 4 of batter and 3 of Streusel. The top layer should be batter, and it should be thin. Bake coffeecake until a toothpick inserted in center comes out clean, about 1 hour. Remove to a rack, and let cool 5 minutes in pan. Turn cake out of pan, and sprinkle with sifted powdered sugar before serving. Yields 12–16 servings.

Jan Townsend Going Home (California)

Raspberry-Cheese Coffeecake

1 (8-ounce) package cream
   cheese, softened
½ cup butter, softened
1 cup sugar
2 large eggs
¼ cup milk
½ teaspoon vanilla extract

1¾ cups all-purpose flour
1 teaspoon baking powder
½ teaspoon baking soda
¼ teaspoon salt
½ cup seedless raspberry
   preserves
3 tablespoons powdered sugar

Beat first 3 ingredients at medium speed with an electric mixer until creamy. Add eggs, milk, and vanilla, beating until smooth. Combine flour and next 3 ingredients; add to cream cheese mixture, beating at low speed until well blended.

Spread batter in a greased and floured 9x13-inch pan. Dollop with preserves and swirl with a knife. Bake at 350° for 25–30 minutes, or until cake begins to leave sides of pan. Cool slightly, then sprinkle with powdered sugar. Cut into squares. Serves 10–12.

Recipe from Western Fields Guest Cottage, Versailles
Sunrise to Sunset in Kentucky (Kentucky)

Chocolate-Sour Cream Coffeecake

CAKE:

1 cup butter or margarine,
   softened
2 cups sugar
2 eggs
1½ cups cake flour

1½ teaspoons baking powder
½ teaspoon salt
1 cup sour cream
½ teaspoon vanilla

Preheat oven to 350°. Cream butter and sugar in a large bowl until fluffy. Add eggs, beating until smooth. In a medium bowl, sift together flour, baking powder, and salt. Gradually add dry ingredients to creamed mixture, blending well. Gently fold in sour cream and vanilla.

TOPPING:

1 cup chopped pecans
2 tablespoons sugar

1 teaspoon cinnamon

Combine ingredients in a small bowl.

CHOCOLATE GLAZE:

¼ cup butter or margarine

½ cup semisweet chocolate chips

Melt butter and chocolate chips in a small saucepan over low heat, stirring until smooth. Sprinkle 2 tablespoons Topping in bottom of greased and floured 9-inch tube pan. Spoon ½ Cake batter into pan. Sprinkle 4 tablespoons Topping over batter, and drizzle ½ cup Glaze over Topping. Spoon remaining batter into pan, and sprinkle with remaining Topping. Reserve remaining Glaze. Bake 1 hour to 1 hour 15 minutes or until a toothpick inserted in center comes out clean. Cool 10 minutes in pan. Turn onto serving plate. Drizzle remaining Glaze over top of warm cake. Yields about 20 servings.

Favorite Recipes from Our Kitchens to Yours (Michigan)

Almond Apple Coffeecake

⅓ plus ¾ cup sugar, divided
½ cup sliced almonds
   (optional)
2 teaspoons cinnamon
½ cup butter or margarine
2 eggs
1 teaspoon vanilla

2 cups all-purpose flour
1 teaspoon baking powder
1 teaspoon baking soda
½ teaspoon salt
1 cup sour cream
1 medium apple, pared, cored,
   and sliced

Mix together ⅓ cup sugar, almonds, and cinnamon, and set aside. Cream butter, and gradually add remaining ¾ cup sugar; beat until fluffy. Add eggs and vanilla. Sift together flour, baking powder, baking soda, and salt. At low speed, add flour mixture to butter mixture alternately with sour cream, beating well after each addition. Spread ½ of batter in greased and floured Bundt or tube pan. Top with apple slices, and sprinkle with ½ of almond mixture. Pour in remaining batter, and top with remaining almond mixture. Bake at 375° for about 45 minutes. Cool 30 minutes in pan. Serves 16.

Note: Can be baked, then wrapped in foil and frozen—reheated in foil at 350° for 50 minutes. Open foil last 10 minutes.

With Lots of Love (Wyoming)

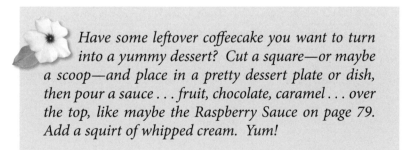

Have some leftover coffeecake you want to turn into a yummy dessert? Cut a square—or maybe a scoop—and place in a pretty dessert plate or dish, then pour a sauce . . . fruit, chocolate, caramel . . . over the top, like maybe the Raspberry Sauce on page 79. Add a squirt of whipped cream. Yum!

Florida Blueberry Streusel Coffeecake

Florida's blueberries are the first to ripen in North America and are large and flavorfully sweet. Blueberries contain vitamins A and C, are a good source of fiber, iron, and potassium, and are high in antioxidants.

TOPPING:

½ cup packed brown sugar
3 tablespoons all-purpose flour
2 teaspoons cinnamon
2 tablespoons butter, softened
¾ cup chopped walnuts

In a small bowl, combine all ingredients for Topping, except nuts, and stir until mixture resembles fine crumbs. Stir in the nuts, and set aside.

BATTER:

½ cup butter, softened
1 cup sugar
2 teaspoons grated lemon rind
3 eggs
2 cups all-purpose flour
1 teaspoon baking powder
1 teaspoon baking soda
½ teaspoon salt
1 cup sour cream
2 cups blueberries

In a large mixing bowl, cream butter until fluffy; add sugar and grated lemon rind, and beat well. Add eggs, one at a time, beating well after each addition. In a bowl, combine dry ingredients. Add flour mixture to the creamed mixture alternately with sour cream, blending well after each addition. Spread Batter into a greased 9x13-inch baking pan. Sprinkle blueberries and then Topping over the Batter. Bake at 350° for 30–35 minutes. Serve warm. Serves 12.

Florida Cook Book (Florida)

Overnight Blueberry Coffeecake

1 egg
½ cup plus 2 tablespoons sugar,
    divided
1¼ cups all-purpose flour
2 teaspoons baking powder
¾ teaspoon salt
⅓ cup milk
3 tablespoons butter or margarine,
    melted
1 cup fresh blueberries

In a mixing bowl beat egg and ½ cup sugar. Combine flour, baking powder, and salt. Add alternately with milk to sugar mixture, beating well after each addition. Stir in butter. Fold in berries. Pour into a greased 8-inch square baking pan. Sprinkle with remaining sugar. Cover, and chill overnight. Remove from refrigerator 30 minutes before baking. Bake at 350° for 30–35 minutes. Serves 9.

Literary Tastes (Alaska)

Night Before Coffeecake

⅔ cup butter or margarine,
    softened
1 cup sugar
½ cup brown sugar
2 eggs
2 cups all-purpose flour
1 teaspoon baking powder
1 teaspoon baking soda
1 teaspoon cinnamon
½ teaspoon salt
1 cup buttermilk
½ cup raisins, nuts, dates, or
    mixture of all three

Cream butter and sugars. Add eggs; mix. Mix together the dry ingredients. Alternately add flour and buttermilk to the creamed mixture. Add fruit and nuts. Pour into greased 9x13-inch pan.

TOPPING:

½ cup brown sugar
1 teaspoon cinnamon
½ cup nuts
1 teaspoon nutmeg

Mix Topping ingredients together, and sprinkle over cake. Cover tightly with foil, and refrigerate overnight.

Remove foil, and bake at 350° for 35–40 minutes. Serves 9–12.

Home at the Range IV (Kansas)

Butterscotch Pecan Rolls

These are sticky buns extraordinaire.

DOUGH:

1 package active dry yeast
¼ cup sugar, white or brown,
   divided
¼ cup warm water
¾ cup lukewarm milk
1 egg

¼ cup soft shortening, butter,
   or margarine
1 teaspoon grated lemon rind
1 teaspoon salt
3½–3¾ cups unbleached
   or bread flour, divided

In a medium-size mixing bowl, dissolve yeast and 1 teaspoon sugar in warm water. Let stand about 5 minutes or until proofed. Add milk, remaining sugar, egg, shortening, rind, salt, and half the flour. Mix until smooth. Add enough remaining flour to handle dough easily. Turn onto a floured board. Knead until smooth and elastic, about 5 minutes. Add small amounts of flour, if necessary. Cover, and let rise until double, about 1 hour. Rising temperature of 85° is best.

FILLING:

2 tablespoons plus ½ cup
   butter or margarine, divided
½ cup sugar mixed with 1
   tablespoon cinnamon

½ cup brown sugar
1 cup pecan halves

Punch dough down, and proceed as follows: Roll dough into a rectangle 9x15 inches. Spread with the 2 tablespoons softened butter, and sprinkle with the cinnamon-sugar mixture. Roll up tightly beginning at wide end. Seal well by pinching the long end. Cut into 18 rolls.

Melt ½ cup butter, and put into 9x13-inch pan. Stir in brown sugar and pecans. Place rolls on top, cut-side-down. Cover, and let rise until double, 45 minutes.

Bake at 375° until rolls are golden brown, about 20 minutes. Turn out onto a large serving dish. Or turn out onto a large cooling rack, cool completely, wrap, and freeze. Makes 18 rolls.

The Fine Art of Holiday Cooking (Connecticut)

Sticky Buns, Breakfast Sweets

Quicky sticky. This is a sure winner for all ages.

⅔ cup brown sugar
⅛ cup water
1 cup chopped pecans or walnuts
5 tablespoons melted butter or
   margarine

2 (10-count) cans buttermilk
   biscuits (tear apart in quarters)
1 teaspoon cinnamon mixed with
   ¼ cup sugar

Mix brown sugar, water, pecans, and butter together. Spread in 9x13-inch pan. Place quartered biscuits on top of this mixture. Sprinkle cinnamon-sugar on top. Bake at 375° for 20 minutes. Turn upside down on a serving dish immediately. Serves 9.

Favorite Recipes from the Foothills of Carefree, Arizona (Arizona)

Val's Famous Firehouse Cinnamon/Orange Rolls

DOUGH:

4 cups milk	2 tablespoons instant yeast
1 cup sugar	2 teaspoons salt
1 cup shortening	4 eggs
4 cups all-purpose flour	

Scald or scold milk (I stand over it and call it bad names). Add sugar and shortening, and continue heating until shortening is melted. Cool slightly. In a large bowl, mix flour, instant yeast and salt. Pour hot milk mixture in with dry ingredients. Mix well. Add 4 eggs, one at a time, mixing well after each.* Allow dough to rise to double. Punch down. Let rise again. On floured counter top, roll dough to oblong strip (approximately 12–14 inches wide, 3 feet long, and ½-inch thick).

CINNAMON FILLING:

1 stick butter or margarine	1 tablespoon cinnamon
2 cups brown sugar	Nuts and raisins (optional)

or ORANGE FILLING:

1 stick butter or margarine	Grated rind of 1 orange
2 cups sugar	Nuts and raisins (optional)

Melt butter or margarine. Pour evenly over Dough. Mix dry ingredients of preferred filling together. Sprinkle over buttered Dough. Roll Dough, and slice to 1-inch-thick slabs. Place on baking pan, and let rise until double in size. Bake 350° for 20–30 minutes, depending on the elevation, humidity, and how hungry the guys are!

VANILLA OR ORANGE FROSTING:

4 cups powdered sugar	Milk for smooth consistency
4 tablespoons butter, softened	
1 teaspoon vanilla or grated orange rind	

(continued)

(Val's Famous Firehouse Cinnamon/Orange Rolls continued)

Blend sugar, butter, and vanilla or orange rind together. Add enough milk to give a smooth consistency. Spread mixture over hot rolls. I stick my CLEAN hand into the frosting, and spread it evenly over the rolls while still hot from the oven. Makes 4–5 dozen rolls.

*If needed, add additional flour, 1 cup at a time, until dough is "sticky"— NOT dry or stiff (4–6 cups will be sufficient). Be careful not to add too much flour (10 cups is too much).

The National Firefighters Recipe Book (Arizona)

Butter Rolls with Caramel Sauce

BUTTER ROLLS:

1½ cups self-rising flour
⅜ teaspoon salt
½ cup plus 2 teaspoons butter,
   divided

¼ cup water
2 tablespoons sugar

Sift flour and salt. Cut in ½ cup butter. Add water, and mix well. Divide into 2 portions. Roll each portion on a lightly floured board. Sprinkle each with 1 tablespoon sugar and dot with 1 teaspoon butter. Fold ends over, and roll lengthwise; cut each into 6 rolls. Place rolls in greased pan, cut side down, and bake at 400° for 20 minutes.

CARAMEL SAUCE:

½ cup plus 2 tablespoons
   butter

2½ cups sugar
2 cups milk, warmed

Melt butter in iron skillet; add sugar. Let brown, then add milk. Stir vigorously and drizzle over warm rolls. Makes 12 rolls.

Lessons from the Lunchroom (Kentucky)

Apple Danish

3 cups plus 2 tablespoons
   all-purpose flour, divided
½ teaspoon salt
1 cup butter-flavored shortening
1 egg
½ cup milk
4 or 5 large Granny Smith
   apples

½ cup raisins
1½ cups sugar
1 teaspoon cinnamon
½ stick margarine, melted
1 egg white, beaten
½ cup powdered sugar
2 tablespoons water

Preheat oven to 375°. Combine 3 cups flour and salt; cut in shortening. Separate egg, and save white for top. Beat yolk with milk, and add to flour mixture; mix well. Grease a 10x15-inch baking pan, and set aside. Divide dough into 2 pieces, and roll each to fit pan. Dough will be very thin.

Peel apples, and slice very thin; add raisins, sugar, cinnamon, melted margarine, and remaining 2 tablespoons flour; stir to mix well. Place first dough layer in pan, and top with apple filling. Cover with remaining layer of dough.

Brush top crust with beaten egg white, and bake 35–40 minutes, or until golden brown. Combine powdered sugar and water; drizzle over warm pastry. Best served warm or at room temperature. Serves 20.

A Carolina Country Collection II (South Carolina)

Best to bake with an apple that holds its shape when cooked in a high-heat dish. The classic choice is the Granny Smith. Another choice is the Pink Lady, which is pear scented and delicious in an apple pie. Galas and Fujis have a medium firmness for muffins and cakes. The Golden Delicious is probably the most all-purpose apple.

Victory Baked Apple Rolls

APPLE LAYER:

3–4 apples, peeled and thinly ¼ cup sugar
   sliced

Combine apples and sugar; set aside.

DOUGH:

1½ cups all-purpose flour   3 tablespoons shortening
3 teaspoons baking powder   ⅓ cup milk
1 teaspoon salt   1 tablespoon butter

Mix first 4 ingredients till crumbly; add milk (add more milk or flour to get roll-out consistency). Roll out on floured board. Spread with Apple Layer, dot with butter, and roll jellyroll-style; cut into rolls.

CINNAMON SAUCE:

¾ cup sugar   ⅛ teaspoon salt
½ cup brown sugar   1 teaspoon cinnamon
⅓ teaspoon nutmeg   2 cups water

Bring ingredients to a boil, and pour into 9x13-inch pan. Place cut rolls in hot Sauce. Bake at 400° for 30 minutes. Serves 12.

Quilter's Delight, Busy Day Recipes (Idaho)

Quick Apple Tarts

Not just for breakfast—good with ice cream, too.

1 cooking apple, peeled and
   chopped
3 tablespoons sugar
2 tablespoons chopped walnuts
2 tablespoons raisins (optional)

¼ teaspoon cinnamon
1 (8-ounce) can refrigerated
   crescent roll dough
3 tablespoons sugar, mixed with
   1 teaspoon cinnamon

Stir together apple, sugar, nuts, raisins, and cinnamon in small bowl; set aside. Separate dough into 8 triangles, stretching slightly. Spoon one heaping tablespoon of apple mixture into center of each triangle. Fold corners over, and pinch edges together to seal. Sprinkle with cinnamon/sugar mixture. Place tarts about one inch apart on ungreased baking sheet. Bake at 350° for 18–20 minutes. Cool tarts about 20 minutes on wire rack before serving. Best served same day. Makes 8.

Wyndmere Community Alumni Cookbook (North Dakota)

Apple Pancake Puff

Great to serve for weekend or overnight guests.

6 eggs
1½ cups milk
1 cup all-purpose flour
2 tablespoons sugar
1 teaspoon vanilla
¼ teaspoon salt
¼ teaspoon cinnamon

⅛ teaspoon nutmeg
½ cup (1 stick) butter or margarine
2 tart green apples, peeled, cored,
 thinly sliced
2 tablespoons brown sugar
¼ cup chopped walnuts or pecans

Preheat oven to 425°. In a blender or processor, mix eggs, milk, flour, sugar, vanilla, salt, cinnamon, and nutmeg. Place butter in a 9x13-inch baking dish; heat in oven until butter is melted, but not brown. Add apple slices, and heat in oven several minutes until they begin to sizzle. Quickly remove from oven, and pour batter over apples all at once; sprinkle with brown sugar and nuts. Return to oven; bake approximately 20 minutes, or until puffed and golden. Cut into squares. Serve immediately. Serves 6 8.

Back Home Again (Indiana)

Ice Cream Strudel

½ pound butter, melted
½ pint vanilla ice cream, softened
2 cups all-purpose flour

1 (16-ounce) jar apricot preserves
Chopped nuts
Raisins (optional)

Melt butter; mix with ice cream and flour, and form into soft ball. Refrigerate at least 1 hour (overnight, if possible).

Divide into 4 parts. Roll each into rectangular sheet on floured surface. Fill with apricot preserves, nuts, and raisins, if desired, and roll like jellyroll.

Place on greased cookie sheet. Slit each roll halfway-down in 10 places. Brush with milk. Bake 45 minutes at 350°. Makes 40 pieces.

The Way to a Man's Heart (Pennsylvania)

Strawberries and Cream Bread

Strawberries and Cream Bread

1¾ cups all-purpose flour
½ teaspoon baking powder
¼ teaspoon baking soda
½ teaspoon salt
¼ teaspoon cinnamon
½ cup butter, softened
¾ cup sugar

2 eggs
½ cup sour cream
1 teaspoon vanilla
1 teaspoon almond extract
1 cup coarsely chopped
   strawberries
¾ cup chopped walnuts

Combine flour, baking powder, baking soda, salt, and cinnamon. In small bowl, cream butter. Gradually add sugar, and beat until light. Beat in eggs, one at a time. Beat in sour cream, vanilla, and almond extract. Stir into flour mixture only until dry ingredients are moistened. Fold in strawberries and nuts. Grease a 4x8-inch loaf pan. Turn mixture into pan. Bake at 350° for 60–65 minutes, or until wooden pick inserted in center comes out clean. Let stand in pan 10 minutes. Turn out onto a rack to cool. Makes 1 loaf.

Pungo Strawberry Festival Cookbook (Virginia)

Cinnamon Surprise

2 (8-count) packages refrigerator
   crescent roll dough
2 tablespoons brown sugar
1 teaspoon sugar

1 teaspoon cinnamon
16 marshmallows
2 tablespoons butter, melted

Separate roll dough on lightly floured surface. Mix brown sugar, sugar, and cinnamon in small bowl. Dip marshmallows one at a time in melted butter; roll in sugar mixture, coating well. Place on crescent roll triangle. Bring up edges to enclose marshmallow, sealing well. Place 2 inches apart on baking sheet. Brush lightly with remaining melted butter. Bake at 375° for 10–13 minutes or until marshmallows melt, leaving rolls with hollow, sweet-coated centers. Serves 16.

Beyond Oats (Colorado)

Streusel Filled Apple Muffins

1½ cups all-purpose flour
2 teaspoons baking powder
¼ cup sugar
½ teaspoon nutmeg
¼ cup vegetable oil
½ cup milk
1 egg, beaten
1 medium apple, peeled and grated

Sift together dry ingredients. Make a well, and pour in oil, milk, egg, and grated apple. Mix only until moistened. Spoon ¾ of batter into well-greased muffin tins. Sprinkle Streusel Filling over each, then top with 1 teaspoon batter. Bake at 350° for 20–25 minutes.

STREUSEL FILLING:
¼ cup brown sugar
1 tablespoon all-purpose flour
½ teaspoon cinnamon
1 tablespoon butter or
  margarine, melted
¼ cup chopped nuts

Combine above ingredients. Yields 1 dozen muffins.

From the Apple Orchard (Missouri)

Cherry Lemon Muffins

1 cup dried cherries
2 cups all-purpose flour, divided
2 teaspoons baking powder
1 teaspoon baking soda
½ teaspoon salt
5 tablespoons sugar
1 egg
1 cup buttermilk
5 tablespoons butter, melted
Juice from 1 lemon
Lemon zest from 1 lemon

Preheat oven to 375°. Place dried cherries (sprinkled with 2 table-spoons flour to separate them) in a food processor. Pulse to chop. In a large bowl, sift together remaining flour, baking powder, baking soda, salt, and sugar. In another bowl, lightly beat the egg. Add buttermilk, butter, lemon juice, and zest. Combine well. Add chopped cherries. Stir buttermilk mixture into flour mixture just until dry ingredients are moistened. Pour into greased muffin tins. Bake 20 minutes or until muffins are golden brown. Makes 12.

Tried and True Recipes (Virginia)

Chunky Monkey Muffins

1 cup walnuts

Preheat oven to 350°. Toast walnuts in oven, then coarsely chop, and set aside. Prepare muffin papers for 16 muffins. Set pans aside.

CREAM CHEESE FILLING:

4 ounces cream cheese, softened	**Pinch of salt**
2 tablespoons powdered sugar	**½ cup semisweet chocolate chips**

Combine and cream well the cream cheese, powdered sugar, and salt. Blend in chocolate chips. Set aside.

MUFFIN BATTER:

2 cups all-purpose flour	**2 tablespoons oil**
1 cup sugar	**1 large egg**
½ teaspoon salt	**½ cup orange juice**
1 teaspoon baking powder	**2 large bananas, peeled**
1 teaspoon baking soda	**1 teaspoon vanilla**

In a bowl, sift dry ingredients. Add chopped nuts. Set aside. In mixer bowl, blend oil, egg, orange juice, bananas, and vanilla. Slowly add dry ingredients, and blend. Divide batter evenly between prepared muffin cups, reserving a small amount. Top each muffin with a teaspoon of Cream Cheese Filling, and press down slightly. Put a small amount of reserved batter on top of each muffin to cover cream cheese. Bake at 350° for 20–25 minutes.

Recipe by Kangaroo House B&B, Orcas Island
Another Taste of Washington State (Washington)

Orange Raisin Scones with Orange Butter

Scones are a great alternative to muffins for breakfast. These are particularly popular, and the orange butter enhances the flavor of the scones. Outstanding!

1¾ cups all-purpose flour	**⅓ cup butter**
3 tablespoons sugar	**½ cup golden raisins**
2½ teaspoons baking powder	**2 eggs, used separately**
2 teaspoons grated orange peel	**4–6 tablespoons half-and-half**

Preheat oven to 400°. In medium bowl, combine flour, sugar, baking powder, and orange peel. Cut in butter until crumbly. Stir in raisins, 1 egg, lightly beaten, and enough half-and-half to just moisten mixture.

Turn dough onto lightly floured surface; knead lightly 10 times. Roll into 9-inch circle. Cut into 8–12 wedges. Place on cookie sheet one inch apart. Brush with remaining beaten egg. Bake 10–12 minutes or until golden brown. Immediately remove from cookie sheet.

ORANGE BUTTER:

½ cup butter, softened	**2 tablespoons orange marmalade**

Make Orange Butter by mixing together butter and marmalade until combined. Serve with warm scones. Makes 8–12 scones.

Recipe from Courthouse Square Bed & Breakfast, Crandon
Have Breakfast with Us . . . Again (Wisconsin)

Orange Raisin Scones
with Orange Butter

Old-Fashioned Jelly Roll

¾ cup cake flour
¾ teaspoon baking powder
¼ teaspoon salt
4 eggs

¾ cup sugar
1 teaspoon vanilla
Powdered sugar for dusting
1 cup tart red jelly

Sift flour then measure. Combine baking powder, salt, and eggs in bowl. Beat with egg beater (or whisk), adding sugar gradually until mixture becomes thick and light colored. Gradually fold in flour, then vanilla. Turn into 10x15-inch pan, which has been lined with parchment paper, then greased. Bake in 400° oven for 13 minutes or until done. Turn cake out on cloth or towel, dusted with powdered sugar. Quickly remove paper, and cut off crisp edges of cake. Roll, and wrap in cloth. Let cool about 10 minutes, unroll, spread cake with jelly, and roll again. Wrap in cloth; place on cake rack to finish cooling. Serves 10–12.

Amish Country Cookbook I (Indiana)

Pistol Packin' Mama Pecan Cups

Fun and impressive to bake and take.

3 ounces cream cheese, softened
½ cup plus 2 tablespoons butter
  or margarine, softened,
  divided
1 cup all-purpose flour

2 eggs
1 cup brown sugar
1 teaspoon vanilla
Dash of salt
1 cup broken pecans, divided

Mix cream cheese and ½ cup butter. Blend into flour with fork. Chill 1 hour or longer. Shape into 1-inch balls. Press in tiny muffin tins (12 to a tin). Combine eggs, brown sugar, remaining 2 tablespoons butter, vanilla, and salt. Beat until smooth. Divide pecans in half. Use ½ to sprinkle on bottom of each cup. Add filling, and top with remaining pecans. Bake at 325° for 25 minutes. Remove quickly before filling hardens. Makes 24.

Cowboy Cookin' (Arizona)

List of Contributors

Chocolate Yule Log, page 176

Listed below are the cookbooks that have contributed recipes to *Recipe Hall of Fame Guilty Pleasures*, along with copyright, author, publisher, city, and state. The information in parentheses indicates the BEST OF THE BEST cookbook in which the recipe originally appeared.

Aliant Cooks for Education ©2004 Morris Press Cookbooks, Alexander City, AL (Alabama)

Amish Country Cookbook I ©1979 Evangel Publishing House, Nappanee, IN (Indiana)

Angel Food, by Norma Johnson, Pinehurst, NC (North Carolina)

Another Taste of Washington State ©2000 Tracy Winters, Greensburg, IN (Washington)

Aspic and Old Lace ©1987 The Northern Indiana Historical Society, South Bend, IN (Indiana)

At the End of the Fork, by Barbara Roberts, Snellville, GA (Georgia)

Aunt Bee's Delightful Desserts ©1996 by Ken Beck and Jim Clark, Nashville, TN (Tennessee)

Aunty Pua's Keiki Cookbook ©1991 by Ann Kondo Corum, Honolulu, HI (Hawaii)

Back Home Again ©1993 The Junior League of Indianapolis, Inc., Indianapolis, IN (Indiana)

The Best of Mayberry ©1996 by Betty Conley Lyerly, Mount Airy, NC (North Carolina)

The Best of the Zucchini Recipes Cookbook ©1992 by E. B. Dandar, by Sterling Specialties Cookbooks, Penndel, PA (Pennsylvania)

Beyond Loaves and Fishes, by St. Paul's Episcopal Churchwomen, Artesia, NM (New Mexico)

Beyond Oats: A Horse Lovers Cookbook © by Arabian Horse Trust, Westminster, CO (Colorado)

The Black Hat Chef Cookbook ©1991 by Richard P. Brisson, by Chef René, Philadelphia, PA (Pennsylvania)

Blueberry Pride: Blueberry Bash Recipes 1989–1993 ©1993 Unalaska Pride, Unalaska, AK (Alaska)

Boardin' in the Thicket ©1990 Wanda A. Landrey, Denton, TX (Texas)

By Request ©1998 Betsy Mann / Photos ©1998 Northland Publishing, Flagstaff, AZ (Arizona)

California Kosher ©1991 Women's League of Adat Ari El, North Hollywood, CA (California)

California Sizzles ©1992 The Junior League of Pasadena, Inc., Pasadena, CA (California)

Call to Post ©1997 Lexington Hearing & Speech Center, Lexington, KY (Kentucky)

Calling All Cooks ©1982 Junior League of Mobile, Inc., by Telephone Pioneers of America, Alabama Chapter #34, Birmingham, AL (Alabama)

Cardinal Country Cooking, by School District of Brodhead Playground Committee, Brodhead, WI (Wisconsin)

A Carolina Country Collection II, by Pat Turner, Seneca, SC (South Carolina)

Causing a Stir, by Junior League of Dayton, OH (Ohio)

Centennial Cookbook, by Second Presbyterian Church, Racine, WI (Wisconsin)

A Century of Mormon Cookery, Volume I ©2002 Horizon Publishers & Distributors, by Hermine B. Horman, Bountiful, UT (Utah)

Chattanooga Cook Book ©1970 Helen McDonald Exum, TN (Tennessee)

Christ Reformed Church Historical Cookbook, Martinsburg, WV (West Virginia)

Church Family Recipes, by Carson Valley United Methodist Church, Gardnerville, NV (Nevada)

A Collection of My Favorite Recipes, by Deette Daniels, Meadville, MS (Mississippi)

Come and Dine ©1986 Naomi Fonville, Lumberton, MS (Mississippi)

Come, Dine With Us!, by The Gravenor's, Salisbury, MD (Mid-Atlantic)

Cook Book, by Mary Martha Society of Redeemer Lutheran Church, Chico, CA (California)

The Cookbook AAUW, by American Association of University Women, Jamestown, NY (New York)

Cookie Exchange ©1994 Georgie Ann Patrick and Cynthia Ann Duncan, Greenley, CO (Colorado)

Cookin' to Beat the Band, by Tri Kappa, Elkhart, IN (Indiana)

Cooking at Thimbleberry Inn, by Sharon Locey, Bayfield, WI (Wisconsin)

Cooking with Love & Memories, by Corinth Baptist Church WOM, Monroe, NC (North Carolina)

Cooking with My Friends ©2003 by LaVece Ganter Hughes, Nicholasville, KY (Kentucky)

Country Cupboard, by Lois Kruegar, Washington Island, WI (Wisconsin)

Cowboy Cookin' ©1990 Sharon Wilson Walton, Cave Creek, AZ (Arizona)

The Dexter Cider Mill Apple Cookbook ©1995 Katherine Merkel Koziski, Chelsea, MI (Michigan)

Dining by Design ©1999 Junior League of Pasadena, Inc., Pasadena, CA (California)

Dining on Deck ©1986 Linda Vail, Charlotte, VT (New England)

Down Home Cooking Done Right, by New Life Women's Leadership Project, Williamston, NC (North Carolina)

Dutch Pantry Simply Sweets, by Dutch Pantry Family Restaurant, Williamstown, WV (West Virginia)

Faithfully Charleston ©2001 St. Michael's Episcopal Church, Charleston, SC (South Carolina)

Family Favorites, by Catholic Daughters of the Americas #2388, Westlake, LA (Louisiana)

Family Treasures, by First United Methodist Church, Marion, SC (South Carolina)

The Farmington Cookbook ©1986 Farmington Historic House Museum, Louisville, KY (Kentucky)

Favorite Island Cookery Book II and *III*, by Honpa Hongwanji Hawaii Betsuin, Honolulu, HI (Hawaii)

Favorite Recipes from Associated Women for Harding, Searcy, AR (Arkansas)

Favorite Recipes from Our Kitchens to Yours, by Women's Ministries of Michiana Christian Embassy, Niles, MI (Michigan)

Favorite Recipes from the Foothills of Carefree, Arizona, by Our Lady of Joy Catholic Church, Carefree, AZ (Arizona)

Favorite Recipes Home-Style, by Vernon B. Harmon, Jr., Pocahontas, TN (Tennessee)

Feeding His Flock, by Decatur United Methodist Church Women, Decatur, MS (Mississippi)

Fessin' Up with Bon Appétit ©1992 Sue W. Fess, Shreveport, LA (Louisiana)

50 Years and Still Cookin', by Christ Child Society of Akron, OH (Ohio)

The Fine Art of Holiday Cooking ©1992 University of Connecticut, Storrs, CT (New England)

Fine Dining Tennessee Style ©2000 by John M. Bailey, Brandon, MS (Tennessee)

Fishin' for a Cure ©2002 Mt. Carmel United Methodist Church, Benton, KY (Kentucky)

The Flavors of Mackinac ©1997 Mackinac Island Medical Center, Mackinac Island, MI (Michigan)

Florida Cook Book ©2001 Golden West Publishers, Phoenix, AZ (Florida)

Food for the Flock Volume II, by Youngs Chapel Cumberland Presbyterian Church, Kingston, TN (Tennessee)

Food for Thought ©2005 Alzheimer's Association, Toledo, OH (Ohio)

From Our Home to Yours ©2003 by Lisa Shively Cookbooks, Eden, NC (North Carolina)

From the Apple Orchard ©1984 Leona N. Jackson, Maryville, MO (Missouri)

G.W. Carver Family Recipes, by G.W. Carver Elementary School, Salem, VA (Virginia)

German Recipes ©1994 Penfield Press, Iowa City, IA (Iowa)

Gingerbread...and all the Trimmings ©1987 Waxahachie Junior Service League, Inc., Waxahachie, TX (Texas)

Good Food From Michigan ©1995 Laurie Woody, Grawn, MI (Michigan)

Good Things to Eat, by Lynn Tritremmel, Hamilton, NJ (Mid-Atlantic)

Grandma Mamie Jones' Family Favorites, by Marilyn B. Jones, Climax, GA (Georgia)

A Gracious Plenty, by Christ Episcopal Church, Bluefield, WV (West Virginia)

A Great Taste of Arkansas ©1986 Southern Flavors, Inc., Pine Bluff, AR (Arkansas)

Gritslickers ©2005 by Lisa Shively Cookbooks, Eden, NC (North Carolina)

A Hancock Community Collection, by The Guild, Hancock, NH (New England)

Have Breakfast with Us…Again ©1995 Amherst Press, Amherst, WI (Wisconsin)

Heavenly Delights, by Sacred Heart Altar Society, Nelson, NE (Great Plains)

Heavenly Helpings, by Fort Gay United Methodist Church Women, Fort Gay, WV (West Virginia)

Heirloom Recipes and By Gone Days ©1993 Heirloom Enterprises, by Sherry Maurer, Zoar, OH (Ohio)

Home at the Range IV, by Chapter EX. P.E.O., Oakley, KS (Great Plains)

Home at/on the Range with Wyoming BILS, by Wyoming/PEO Sisterhood, Chapter Y, Casper, WY (Big Sky)

Home Cookin' is a Family Affair, by Windsor Junior Women's Club, Windsor, CT (New England)

The Hudson River Valley Cookbook ©1995, 1998 Waldy Malouf, Boston, MA (New York)

Hungry for Home: Stories of Food from Across the Carolinas ©2003 by Amy Rogers, Winston-Salem, NC (North Carolina)

In the Kitchen with Kate ©1995 Capper Press, Inc., Topeka, KS (Great Plains)

Irene's Country Cooking: From Farm to Freeway ©2002 by Irene D. Wakefield, Cheyenne, WY (Big Sky)

J. Bildner & Sons Cookbook ©1993 James L. Bildner, Boston, MA (New England)

Jambalaya ©1983 Junior League of New Orleans, Inc., New Orleans, LA (Louisiana)

Jan Townsend Going Home ©1996 Janice Lynn Townsend, Auburn, CA (California)

Jefferies Relay Team: Generating a Cure ©2005 The Jefferies Relay for Life Team, Moncks Corner, SC (South Carolina)

Kitchen Komforts ©2003 Three Hearts Snacks, Inc., by Lulu Roman, Nashville, TN (Tennessee)

La Bonne Louisiane ©1983 Michelle M. Odom, Baton Rouge, LA (Louisiana)

Lessons from the Lunchroom, by Jennifer Nelson, Morton's Gap, KY (Kentucky)

Let's Say Grace Cookbook, by Mrs. Mary Bridler, Mobile, AL (Alabama)

Lighthouse Secrets ©1999 The Junior Service League of St. Augustine, Inc., St. Augustine, FL (Florida)

Literary Tastes, by Friends of the Haines Borough Public Library, Haines, AK (Alaska)

Merrymeeting Merry Eating ©Regional Memorial Hospital, Brunswick, ME (New England)

Minnie Pearl Cooks ©1970 Minnie Pearl, Nashville, TN (Tennessee)

Mom-Mom's Cookbook ©2001 Marilyn Hudson, Monterville, WV (West Virginia)

Montezuma Amish Mennonite Cookbook I and *II*, by Mrs. Ruth Yoder, Montezuma, GA (Georgia)

Moosewood Restaurant Book of Desserts ©1997 The Moosewood Collective, Ithaca, NY (New York)

More…Home Town Recipes, by South Fork Volunteer Fire Department, Inc., Brandywine, WV (West Virginia)

My Favorite Maryland Recipes ©1964 Helen Avalynne Tawes, Centreville, MD (Mid-Atlantic)

The National Firefighters Recipe Book, by Candice M. DeBarr and Louis A. DePasquale, Austin, TX (Arizona)

90th Anniversary Trinity Lutheran Church Cookbook, Great Bend, KS (Great Plains)

Nome Centennial Cookbook 1898–1998 ©1996 by Kay Hansen, Homer, AK (Alaska)

Nutbread and Nostalgia ©1919 The Junior League of South Bend, Inc., South Bend, IN (Indiana)

Ohio Cook Book ©2002 Golden West Publishers, by Donna Goodrich, Phoenix, AZ (Ohio)

Ohio State Grange Cookbook, by Ohio State Grange, Fredericktown, OH (Ohio)

The Old Yacht Club Inn Cookbook, by Nancy Donaldson, Santa Barbara, CA (California)

Only the Best, by Gayle Holdman, Highland, UT (Utah)

Open House: A Culinary Tour ©2002 Junior League of Murfreesboro, TN (Tennessee)

Our Best Home Cooking ©1993 Pend Oreille County Historical Society, Newport, WA (Washington)

Our Daily Bread, and Then Some..., by The Eldred Family Home School, Auburn, NY (New York)

Outdoor Cooking: From Backyard to Backpack ©1991 Department of Transportation, State of Arizona, Phoenix, AZ (Arizona)

The Parkview Way to Vegetarian Cooking, by Parkview Memorial Hospital Auxiliary, Brunswick, ME (New England)

Perennials ©1984 Junior League of Gainesville-Hall County, Inc., Gainesville, GA (Georgia)

Peter Christian's Recipes ©1983 by Shirley Edes, Julia Philipson and Murray Washburn, Camden, ME (New England)

The Philadelphia Orchestra Cookbook ©1980 West Philadelphia Women's Committee for the Philadelphia Orchestra, Bryn Mawr, PA (Pennsylvania)

A Pinch of Rose & A Cup of Charm ©1998 by Rose Dorchuck, Kosciusko, MS (Mississippi)

The Pink Lady...In the Kitchen, By Medical Center of South Arkansas Auxiliary, El Dorado, AR (Arkansas)

Pirate's Pantry ©1976 Junior League of Lake Charles, Inc., Gretna, LA (Louisiana)

Prescriptions for Good Eating ©1984 Greenville County Medical Society Auxiliary, Greenville, SC (South Carolina)

Pungo Strawberry Festival Cookbook, Virginia Beach, VA (Virginia)

The Pure Food Club of Jackson Hole ©2001 by Judy S. Clayton, Jackson Hole, WY (Big Sky)

The Queen Victoria® Cookbook ©1992 by Joan and Dane Wells, Cape May, NJ (Mid-Atlantic)

Quilter's Delight, Busy Day Recipes, by Lemhi Piece Makers, Salmon, ID (Idaho)

Racing to the Table: A Culinary Tour of Sporting America ©2002 The Blood Horse, Inc., by Margaret Guthrie, Lexington, KY (Kentucky)

Raspberry Enchantment House Tour Cookbook, by Carrie Tingley Hospital Foundation, Albuquerque, NM (New Mexico)

Recipes & Remembrances, by Moab Area Chamber of Commerce, Moab, UT (Utah)

Recipes and Remembrances, by GFWC Santa Rosa Woman's Club, Gulf Breeze, FL (Florida)

Recipes for Lori's Lighthouse, by Lori's Lighthouse Youth Center, Cantonment, FL (Florida)

Recipes from Iowa with Love ©1981 New Boundary Concepts, Inc., by Peg Hein and Kathryn Cramer, Prior Lake, MN (Iowa)

Recipes from Our House, by Assistance League of Denver, CO (Colorado)

Recipes from the Heart, by United Methodist Women of Cumberland United Methodist Church, Florence, SC (South Carolina)

Recipes from the Heart, by St. Mark Lutheran Church and Preschool, Elko, NV (Nevada)

Recipes to Make You Purr, by Humane Society of Park County, Cody, WY (Big Sky)

Red Pepper Fudge and Blue Ribbon Biscuits ©1995 by Amy Rogers, Winston-Salem, NC (North Carolina)

The Ruby Valley Friendship Club Cookbook II, by Ruby Valley Friendship Club, Ruby Valley, NV (Nevada)

San Francisco Flavors ©1999 Junior League of San Francisco/Photographs, Jonelle Weaver/Illustrations Kelli Bailey, San Francisco, CA (California)

San Juan Classics II Cookbook ©1998 Dawn Ashbach and Janice Veal, Anacortes, WA (Washington)

Sand in My Shoes ©1990 by Jeannine B. Browning, Melbourne, FL (Florida)

Sandlapper Cooks ©1998 Sandlapper Society, Inc., Lexington, SC (South Carolina)

Sandy Hook Volunteer Fire Co. Ladies Aux. Cookbook, Sandy Hook, CT (New England)

Second Round: Tea-Time at the Masters® ©1988 Junior League of Augusta, GA (Georgia)

Sharing Our Best ©1996 Eagle Historical Society & Museums, Eagle, AK (Alaska)

Sharing Our Best-Franklin ©2002 Franklin Community Church, Franklin, TN (Tennessee)

The Shoalwater's Finest Dinners ©1991 Harris & Friedrich, Seaview, WA (Washington)

Sleigh Bells and Sugarplums ©1992 by Frances A. Gillette and Daughters, Yacolt, WA (Washington)

Something Special Cookbook, by Areline Bolerjack, Enid, OK (Oklahoma)

A Southern Collection: Then and Now ©1994 Junior League of Columbus, GA, Inc., Columbus, GA (Georgia)

St. Ambrose "On the Hill" Cookbook, by St. Ambrose Church, St. Louis, MO (Missouri)

St. Mary's Family Cookbook, by St. Mary's Council of Catholic Women, Bloomington, WI (Wisconsin)

Still Cookin' After 70 Years, by Grace Community Church, Boulder, NV (Nevada)

Sunrise to Sunset in Kentucky ©2000 by Tracy Winters, Greensburg, IN (Kentucky)

The Table at Grey Gables ©1998 by Linda Brooks Jones, Nashville, TN (Tennessee)

Tangier Island Girl, by Patsy Parks Young and Shirley Parks Taylor, Parksley, VA (Virginia)

A Taste of Boston ©1990 Gillian Drake and Terrence Gavan, Provincetown, MA (New England)

Taste of Clarkston: Tried & True Recipes, by Clarkston Area Chamber of Commerce, Clarkston, MI (Michigan)

A Taste of Provincetown ©1991 Gillian Drake, Provincetown, MA (New England)

Taste of the Town, by News Channel 5, Nashville, TN (Tennessee)

The Tea Table ©2003 by Shelley and Bruce Richardson, Perryville, KY (Kentucky)

Three Rivers Renaissance Cookbook IV ©2000 Child Health Association of Sewickley, PA (Pennsylvania)

Tony Clark's New Blueberry Hill Cookbook ©1990 Arlyn Patricia Hertz and Anthony Clark, Camden, ME (New England)

Top O' the Morning ©1992 Alabama Gas Corporation, by Chef Clayton Sherrod, Birmingham, AL (Alabama)

Treasured Favorites ©2001 Disciple Women of First Christian Church, Montgomery, AL (Alabama)

Treat Yourself to the Best Cookbook ©1984 Junior League of Wheeling, WV (West Virginia)

Tried and True by Mothers of 2's, by Westshore Mothers of Twins Club, Westlake, OH (Ohio)

Tried and True Recipes, by Joan Dimengo, Centreville, VA (Virginia)

Vintage Vicksburg ©1985 Junior Auxiliary of Vicksburg, Inc., Vicksburg, MS (Mississippi)

Virginia City Alumni Association Cookbook, by Historic Fourth Ward School Museum, Virginia City, NV (Nevada)

Virginia Wine Country ©1987 Hilde Gabriel Lee and Allen E. Lee, Charlottesville, VA (Virginia)

Wandering & Feasting ©1996 Board of Regents of Washington State University, by Mary Houser Caditz, Pullman, WA (Washington)

Wapiti Meadow Bakes, by Diana Swift, Wapiti Meadow Ranch, Cascade, ID (Idaho)

The Way to a Man's Heart, by Beth Israel Sisterhood, Washington, PA (Pennsylvania)

Welcome Home, by Sisters of Martha & Mary Society, Eagle River, AK (Alaska)

What's Cookin' in Melon County, by Rocky Ford Chamber of Commerce, Rocky Ford, CO (Colorado)

The When You Live in Hawaii You Get Very Creative During Passover Cookbook, by Cookbook Committee, Congregation of Ma'arav, Honolulu, HI (Hawaii)

With Lots of Love ©2002 Taydie Drummond, Cheyenne, WY (Big Sky)

Wyndmere Community Alumni Cookbook, by Wyndmere Community Center, Wyndmere, ND (Great Plains)

Y Cook? ©1994 The Fargo-Moorhead YMCA, Fargo, ND (Great Plains)

A Year of Teas at the Elmwood Inn ©2001 by Shelley and Bruce Richardson, Perryville, KY (Kentucky)

Index

Eggnog Pound Cake, page 41